W9-AHD-164

The Ex-Wives' Guide to Divorce

The Ex-Wives' Guide to

Divorce

How to Navigate Everything from Heartache and Finances to Child Custody

By Holiday Miller and Valerie Shepherd

With some support from
Carol S. Baskin, Esq., and Sheri M. Siegel, PhD

Skyhorse Publishing

Skyhorse Publishing books may be purchased in bulk at special discounts for sales promotion, corporate gifts, fund-raising, or educational purposes. Special editions can also be created to specifications. For details, contact the Special Sales Department, Skyhorse Publishing, 307 West 36th Street, 11th Floor, New York, NY 10018 or info@skyhorsepublishing.com.

Visit our website at www.skyhorsepublishing.com.

10 9 8 7 6 5 4 3 2 1

Library of Congress Cataloging-in-Publication Data

Names: Miller, Holiday, author.
Shepherd, Valerie C., 1973- author.
Title: The ex-wives' guide to divorce : how to navigate everything from heartache and finances to child custody / Holiday Miller, Valerie Shepherd.
Description: New York : Skyhorse Publishing, 2016.
Identifiers: LCCN 2016016585
ISBN 9781510704060 (hardback)
ISBN 9781510704077 (ebook)
Subjects: LCSH: Self-actualization (Psychology)
BISAC: SELF-HELP / Personal Growth / General.
Classification: LCC BF637.S4 M54744 2016
DDC 646.70086/53–dc23 LC record available at https://lccn.loc.gov/2016016585

Cover design by Jane Sheppard
Cover photo credit: istockphoto

Print ISBN: 978-1-5107-0406-0
Ebook ISBN: 978-1-5107-0407-7

Printed in the United States of America

We would like to dedicate this book to all the amazing ex-wives out there.
You inspire us.
We also dedicate this book to our ex-husband.
You clearly have great taste in women.

Contents

Meet the Ex-Wives

Are you shocked to be holding a "divorce" book in your hands? Does the thought of getting a divorce or being an ex-wife completely freak you out? Do you have a giant knot in the pit of your stomach? We can relate because we've been there, signed the papers, and have the *many* stories to prove it. Welcome to the club, girlfriend. The Ex-Wives Club. But don't worry. Our club isn't the kind that requires you to wear pink on Wednesdays or exclude those happily-ever-after friends who still have *Mrs.* in front of their names. In fact, our "Club" is quite the opposite; it's all about supporting each other.

You see, we ex-wives must stick together, which is exactly why we wrote this book.

Even though we are both ex-wives, what you might not know is this: **we married AND divorced the SAME MAN.** Yep, ex-wives to the *exact same man*. And now we're friends. Really, *really* good friends. In fact, we're such good friends we decided to write a book together, the same book you are now holding in your probably sweaty palms. A book charged to help women survive divorce.

Go ahead and let that sink in for a minute. . . . Get the "Ohhh my!" out of the way. Some may call it crazy. We call it brilliant. Valerie (ex-wife #1) married our ex straight out of college. Sooner rather than later they divorced. A few years after their divorce, Holiday (ex-wife #2) met and married said ex. Eventually they divorced as well. But our ex really has nothing to do with our story. You, dear girlfriend, on the other hand, *do*.

Though the path to friendship took some time, we believe our meeting was fated and it was simply divine destiny. Valerie's motto is "Always the bride, never the bridesmaid." Divorced three times, she is a self-proclaimed divorce expert. She's been there, done that, has a closet full of "I got divorced and all I got was this lousy T-shirt" T-shirts.

Holiday has been divorced once, and has made it her goal to learn from the mistakes of those around her (namely Valerie—who was more than happy to share her long list of "Don'ts"). These "Don'ts" not only helped Holiday during her divorce, but equally as important helped her get on the right path towards eventually finding another "I Do!"

Sure, there are plenty of women in the world who share ex-husbands, but what are the chances of them becoming great friends? Now that is rare. So, how did we meet? Thanks to social media. We give all credit to the one and only Facebook.

Our connection began while we were both happily (well, kinda) married. During a random night of Facebook friend searches, Holiday and her husband "found" Valerie. Because Holiday was aware of their similarities (tall blondes, same initial college, same major, same sorority, both Junior League members . . . you get the drift), she sent a short and sweet introductory message. After a few email exchanges, it was clear the ex had married almost the same gal twice.

And how could you not like someone who was almost just like you? Had we met under any other circumstances we would have been buying BFF necklaces.

The Similarities We Share:

- We attended the same college and pledged the same sorority.
- We eventually transferred to different colleges.
- We graduated with degrees in education.
- We now live in the Atlanta area and are active in our local Junior League chapters.
- After some real-world experience, we both chose the self-employed route.
- We're tall blondes with creative, Type A personalities.
- We were raised in the North and are Yankees by nature; although Southern charm comes naturally, especially when we're wearing pearls.
- **We married and divorced the same man.**

Since we both had children, a play date was organized so we could actually meet in person through a mutual friend at a local park. We're not going to lie; it was awkward, but nonetheless we became friends. Well, at least Facebook friends. From there we shared our lives via posts, family updates, and images of our "picture-perfect" lives. Just like everyone on Facebook, right?

Fast-forward a couple of years, and enter a moment of complete desperation on Holiday's part. She had just separated from her husband days before and was dreading her first weekend sans kiddos. During a bubble bath (complete with wine and iPad), she sent Valerie an SOS Facebook message.

"You might possibly be the only person on the planet who could understand the hell I'm in right now. Would it be okay if I call you? Or, how about meeting for lunch, or a drink, or both?"

Valerie took only a millisecond to respond. Both being mothers to little ones, and having so much in common, Valerie wanted to do what she could to help. She didn't even care that they shared an ex. This was clearly a woman reaching out in need, big time. When Holiday didn't respond immediately to Valerie's email, Valerie quickly searched her ex-husband's relationship status. It had changed from "Married" to "Single." The picture of their happy family on the beach was removed. Valerie knew instantly what Holiday was experiencing. The "Big D." Divorce.

Little did Holiday know, Valerie was also in the middle of a stomach-twisting divorce . . . only she was a few months ahead of Holiday in the process.

While speaking with Holiday the next day and hearing the details of what prompted her to reach out, Valerie, without really thinking it through, extended an invitation for Holiday to join her for the weekend. Her advice? Bring a notebook and pen; she was going to tell her everything she needed to know about getting divorced. Holiday quickly accepted the offer. Because, to paraphrase Hippocrates, desperate times called for desperate measures. Holiday arrived on Valerie's doorstep the next evening, with notebook, pen, wine, and cheese in hand.

Valerie felt an overwhelming desire to help Holiday and prepare her for what was to come. Making several mistakes during the beginning stages of her (third) divorce, she wanted to do what she could to help Holiday avoid them. She knew how much pain these mistakes had and would cost her in the unforeseeable future. Feeling that if she had the chance to save just one person from the pain, and from the mistakes she was experiencing, other ex-wife or not, it was her duty as a woman to do so. Holiday eagerly listened, soaking up Valerie's knowledge and experience like a sponge. The bond of friendship was instant, and the rest is history.

And we both bought BFF necklaces the very next day. (Umm, no. Hello . . . we were both getting divorced and on tight budgets!) However, our friendship did blossom. Seven months later we took our first vacation together. Yes, you read that correctly. We did what most women who share an ex-husband would NEVER do together. We loaded up Valerie's ol' grocery-getter SUV with all the kids and headed to the beach for Memorial Day.

The idea of writing a divorce guide together was born during this trip. As Type A women, we both revealed we had massive files, binders, and notebooks filled with documents from our divorces. We both independently googled our little broken hearts away, searching for an organizational tool to help, but came up blank. With few to no available options, we each created our own. Which led us to this conclusion: If we had both run into the same problem, how many other women out there were in the same boat? As women we trusted our shiny, happy wedding planners to get us down the aisle. Where was the equally as shiny (but maybe not as happy) divorce planner we had been looking for? Nowhere to be found, until we created our own.

The Ex-Wives' Guide to Divorce was Born

Regardless of where you are in the process of divorce, there are a few things you need to know. You might think your story is completely unique, and no one has ever gone through what you are going through. We're here to tell you that you're not alone. Even though your circumstances may be different, there's one underlying factor here. Divorce is not fun. Some might even go so far as to say it *sucks.*

Divorce is the death of a dream. It's the dissolution of what was *supposed* to be a lifelong commitment. Whether it's you, your friend, sister, mother, daughter, tennis partner, or any other woman in your life, the process of divorce is not easy. It's painful, emotional, and by far one of the hardest things you will experience in your life. But you *will* get through it. We wrote this book because it's exactly what we wish we had when we were going through it.

If there's one piece of advice we give to women facing divorce, and we will continue to do so this entire book so take note now, it's to ***be prepared***. We definitely learned that the hard way. If you're armed with an organizational tool, knowledge, proper expectations, a map of where you're headed, and the optimistic mantra "This too shall pass," the process of divorce is manageable. Sprinkle in a little humor and love from us, as well as this book, and it might even be manageable plus.

Welcome to the Ex-Wives' Guide!

Our ultimate goal in creating this tool was to help women navigate through what will be one of the most difficult times of their lives. If anything, the *Ex-Wives' Guide to Divorce* will give you the ability to laugh, which, trust us, girlfriend, you will definitely need during this period of darkness.

So grab a pen, take a deep breath, and repeat after us: This too shall pass.

It's time to put your big girl panties on and get down to business!

(You will read the phrase "This too shall pass" and "Time to put your big girl panties on" about forty-seven times each in this book. We counted. Well, not really. But probably really close to forty-seven. So get down with the good intentions behind both of these sayings. We promise they come from love and wanting to see you have a little yin and yang of strength and peacefulness at a time when we know you need it more than ever.)

First, a disclaimer: *The Ex-Wives' Guide to Divorce* was written with one goal in mind: to help women prepare, organize, and navigate effectively through the divorce process. We are not in any way encouraging or suggesting divorce, but rather providing helpful tools and resources. The topics presented in this book have been developed strictly from our personal experiences. Our mission is to share our stories with you so you can avoid making the same mistakes we made. Every situation is different, and only you can be the true judge of your marriage or relationship.

This book does not seek to replace legal advice or licensed professional expertise. We do not make any guarantees regarding results or outcomes in your personal relationship or divorce proceedings. Just like a facial scrub featured in *Glamour* magazine, we are simply sharing our thoughts and experiences. You might get zits. Don't hold us accountable. We can't guarantee a pimple-free future.

Please know that we have collaborated with others who have experienced divorce. Some names and events may have been changed or altered to protect the privacy of those involved.

Our wish for you is to prepare yourself, protect yourself, and remember to love yourself. We sincerely hope you can repair your marriage and restore your fairy tale. If this isn't an option, we hope to give you the tools you will need to effectively go through your divorce.

Regardless of your marital status, we wish you happiness, peace, and a happily ever after.

We are NOT:

- Professional Therapists
- Licensed Counselors
- Relationship or Divorce Specialists (unless personal experience counts!)
- Financial Planners or Specialists
- Attorneys or Legal Advisors
- Behavioral Psychologists
- Professional Mediators
- Child Specialists

We ARE:

- Ex-Wives
- Mothers
- Girlfriends (who LOVE to talk!)
- Entrepreneurs
- Focused on helping women not only *survive divorce*, but take charge of their situation.
- Believers in the kind of love that lasts forever. Fairy tale and all.

First Steps
{knowledge is power}

"Always be prepared."

—The Girl Scouts

While there's really nothing in this world that can entirely prepare you for divorce, we're going to give it our best shot. If you don't read any other chapter in this book besides this one, we feel you've at least been given the "quick-start" overview of what you are in store for. You know, like when you buy that new camera with all the fun filter settings that will make you look thinner, decrease your wrinkles, and make you look thinner (totally worth repeating). It comes with a quick start sheet, because they know you want to dive into the basics right away so the camera will at least function. Because when you first enter or contemplate divorce, the one thing we know you have to be able to do is function.

Knowledge is indeed power, so put your big girl panties on, girlfriend, and let's get started. In our experience, below are the first steps you should consider when contemplating or entering divorce. These aren't baby steps, they're giant steps. But they're giant steps toward the future you need to secure for yourself and the ones you love.

Get Organized

Organization is so important, we dedicated an entire chapter to it (see page 37, "Get Organized, Girl"). There you'll find lists of the paperwork and information you need to collect, as well as tips on keeping it all organized.

We've also created worksheets and checklists you can use to create your very own Divorce Planner, just visit www.exwivesguide.com. Samples of these worksheets can be found in the back of the book.

Finances

First and foremost, save your money. We are channeling both your mother and Suze Orman here. Whatever you do, don't spend money on anything you don't need. If you're anything like us, this might present a challenge; see the samples below to help you define wants versus needs.

WANTS vs. NEEDS

WANT: This season's designer shoes at Nordstrom.
NEED: Shoes for your kids.

WANT: Girls' night out with friends at the chic new restaurant downtown.
NEED: Time with your friends . . . for free. (Key word here is FREE!)

WANT: A mani/pedi
NEED: Money to pay your attorney; he/she won't care how your nails look.

WANT: Your favorite bottle of Pinot Noir from the Willamette Valley.
NEED: Wine. In the box, in a bottle, whatever.

Prepare Financial Documents

Preparing your financial information is tedious and time-consuming. Actually, it's more like super tedious and super time-consuming. But it's the first step in ensuring you receive or pay the right amount of support from/to your spouse. Do not take this lightly! In our experience, every minute spent preparing will save you ten minutes of worrying or scrambling.

Most attorneys will email or send you a financial worksheet to complete. Do your best to fill this out in its entirety prior to your first meeting. You may think it's overkill at first, but take it from us, it's not. This will save you not only time, but also money. And money is what puts a roof over your head and food in your mouth. Many state courts also have a standard financial form available online.

Open a Separate Bank Account and Credit Card ASAP

In addition to gathering financial documents, you'll want to take the necessary precautions to protect yourself. Not only should you save money, but it's time to open a separate bank account. Don't get caught in a financial trap. If you can save money and keep it in a secure account, you'll be prepared for future expenses. Far too many women become trapped by their spouse's control over money, especially in the case of abusive relationships. Don't let this happen to you. It might be the one thing you'll be high-fiving yourself for in years to come.

If possible, open a separate credit card in your name only. This will help establish your credit as well as provide spending flexibility.

The sooner you take these steps the better, especially if your income is significantly less than your spouse's.

Close and/or Freeze Joint Credit Accounts

Sure, a Caribbean vacation would be great right about now, but in reality it will get you into trouble (and we don't mean the fun kind of trouble). To avoid incurring additional joint debt, it's in your best interest to cancel any accounts you share. Some creditors require a balance of zero prior to closing an account. In this case, call and request a freeze; this way no spending or charges will be allowed without your written/verbal consent. In addition, follow up with a signed and dated letter stating your marital status, and again request that a freeze be placed on your credit. Don't forget to file copies of each letter sent for documentation.

Know Your Credit Score

You are entitled to a free credit report every year. Get one now, as in right now. You'll need to settle any disputes and monitor future credit history like a hawk. Remember, knowledge is power. To receive your free credit report, visit www.freecreditreport.com. You will receive a detailed report on your credit history, outstanding debts, etc.

At-A-Glance: Financial Checklist

- Bank Information (monthly statements, deposits, loans, savings, money market and retirement accounts, etc.)
- Income (current family income totals)
- Tax Returns (federal, state, and local)
- Debts (includes mortgage, credit cards, personal loans, etc.)
- Personal Property (list all personal property owned prior to marriage as well as any gifts/inheritance received during marriage)
- Real Estate and Appraisals (list all real estate owned prior to marriage as well as any property purchased during marriage, or received as a gift or inheritance)
- Automobiles
- Wills and Trusts
- Stocks, Bonds, and Mutual Funds
- Safety Deposit Boxes and a detailed list of contents.
- Insurance (health, car, life, disability, etc.)
- Memberships (country clubs, gyms, private groups, etc.)
- Any additional assets you have as an individual and/or couple.

Is This Really Happening?

Divorce is like a bad dream. You're hoping for that moment when you'll wake up and everything will be okay. While we hope this happens for you (and for some of you it will), the reality of the situation is just that. It's really happening.

Chances are you've got the following questions swirling around in your head:

- Is this really happening?
- Is this normal?
- Can I, or more importantly we, fix this?
- Is it really over?
- How and when did it get so bad?
- Am I going to be okay?
- What about the kids?
- What will my family and friends say?
- How am I going to make it on my own?
- Am I being selfish or unreasonable?
- Did he seriously just say what I think he said?
- Did I seriously just say what I think I said?!?
- Will I ever be happy again?
- And many, many more questions

Emotional Management

Emotional management is absolutely crucial during your time of separation/divorce. Don't get ahead of yourself. Take things one step at a time and do your best to think clearly. If you don't keep your emotions in check you will drive yourself (and everyone around you) crazy. And crazy ain't cute. Trust us. One of us tried it. (Notice we didn't specify which one of us.)

Whether you're the one leaving or you're begging him to stay, be prepared for an emotional rollercoaster. And not in the clichéd kind of way, more in the I'm-about-to-take-a-plunge-on-the-tallest-oldest-most-rickety-wooden-rollercoaster-without-a-seatbelt-and-I-think-I-am-going-to-vomit-up-that-crappy-funnel-cake-I-just-ate kind of way.

Divorce is like an onion. There are many layers to the process, and as you peel them back you're bound to shed some serious tears.

With the loops, the twists, the highs, and the lows, it's imperative to keep your emotions in check. We know it's easier said than done, but it's time to hike up those big girl panties a little more and mean business.

In the unfortunate circumstance that your spouse has requested the divorce, you probably feel helpless and abandoned. This is normal, and it sucks—no doubt about it.

For those of you who have made the decision to end your marriage (or perhaps you are in the beginning stages), you're probably experiencing guilt, self-doubt, and fear. Again, this is normal, and it sucks.

The best way to manage your emotions is to be aware of them. Acknowledge them, and consider the true source of your feelings. When you feel an emotion surfacing take a minute to just breathe. Write your feelings down. When you are aware of your emotions you tend to not overreact. Take this from two women who struggled with this. Had we stopped to breathe a little more instead of fuming at others or ourselves, things would have been easier.

We know this is probably going to be one of the hardest times for you during the entire process. Your head, heart, and anything else that helps guide you will be pulled in a million directions. As long as you stay focused on preparing (as well as remaining calm), no matter the outcome of your divorce, you will still be able to keep your head held high.

Surround yourself with people who will encourage you, support you, and love you unconditionally. You need them more than ever now.

Beware: Emotional Rollercoaster

You're going to cry. A lot.
But we promise you'll laugh again.
You're going to get mad. Really mad.
But we promise you'll get through it.
You're going to feel hopeless.
But we promise there is hope.
You're going to feel alone.
But we promise you're not alone. {Hello, Girlfriend!}
You're going to feel scared.
But we promise you're going to be just fine.

Is Your Marriage Really Over?

{*maybe it is, but maybe it isn't*}

"I'm selfish, impatient, and a little insecure. I make mistakes, I'm out of control, and at times hard to handle. But if you can't handle me at my worst, then you sure as hell don't deserve me at my best."

—Marilyn Monroe

I'll never forget the moment I realized my marriage was over. I was recovering from breast augmentation surgery and woke up in the middle of the night with a massive infection. When I called my doctor, he instructed me to get to the hospital immediately. My husband refused to wake up, reminding me this surgery was my choice and the infection was my fault. I knew this was a serious infection. I also knew that if I didn't get to the hospital I was at risk of losing my breast, and possibly my life. As a mother of three, I couldn't take this chance. I drove myself to the ER and was rushed into emergency surgery. Thankfully, I survived, but my breast did not. When I woke up in the recovery room, I realized my husband had not called or visited the hospital to check on me. After waiting several hours, I picked up the phone to tell him I was alive. His response: "I'm fishing." That was the moment I knew our marriage was over.

—Michelle

While some of you may be able to relate directly to Michelle's story, not all of us have had such defining moments when we knew our marriages were over. For Michelle, this experience was the final straw in her decision to file for divorce and finally put an end to her abusive marriage. (She suffered from years of both emotional and physical abuse.) For others, this defining moment may not be so obvious, especially if your spouse is the one requesting the divorce.

So, how do you know if your marriage is really over?

This is a question only you and/or your spouse can answer. Unfortunately, we realize the decision isn't always mutual. Most likely you're reading this book operating from one of these three perspectives:

1. You want a divorce, but he does not.
2. Your spouse wants a divorce, but you do not.
3. The divorce is mutual—you both want it.

Let's get personal and break things down depending on where you stand.

#1: You want a divorce; your spouse does not

Before you go running for the hills, there are a few things you need to know.

Divorce isn't the solution for the following:

- He doesn't give me butterflies anymore.
- I love him, but I'm not "in love" with him.
- We are more like friends than lovers.
- We're just not happy.
- Our life is boring.
- We have grown apart.
- We have the same argument all the time.

If one of the reasons listed above is the main culprit for your divorce, we strongly suggest that you donate this book to your local library, skip the attorney's office, and head straight to a marriage or personal counselor. Maybe you tried counseling but it didn't work. Don't give up just yet. Not all marriage counselors are created equal, and counseling takes time.

Rome wasn't built in a day, and neither was your marriage. It's only fitting that repairing your relationship will take some work, but it's definitely worth the investment in terms of both time and money.

For the record, butterflies will disappear no matter who you're married to. The "in love" feeling lasts an average of two years; friends make better long-term partners than lovers do. And the only person you can blame your boring life on is you. Sorry, girlfriend, these excuses just don't cut it in the divorce arena.

As for the repetitive argument . . . news flash: it doesn't matter who you're married to, you're going to fight about something. We might even take a shot in the dark and guess your arguments revolve around money, sex, or work. Welcome to the club.

While we aren't marriage counselors or experts by any means, what we can tell you is this: the grass isn't always greener. Before you make the final decision to end your marriage, we want to encourage you to do everything you can to save it.

> *My husband and I vowed from day one that divorce was not an option. So I didn't know what to do when the cycles of arguing became nonstop. Both of us were miserable. I suggested marriage counseling; he suggested that we separate and not communicate for a month. This was not what I wanted, but I agreed to it.*
>
> *Although he refused to go to counseling with me, I decided to go alone. I wanted to spend that month fully dedicated to working on our marriage and myself. My counselor helped me to see the situation for what it was, and my role in it. My husband was emotionally checked out and I was initiating arguments in order to get attention and emotions out of him.*
>
> *Even though it was our noncommunication month, one of the terms we set forth in our separation was that we would be allowed to email if it was an important issue or something constructive. Every time I went to counseling I sent him an email to let him know what I learned, how I felt, and what I took away that I thought might help our marriage. Not once did he email me back. Not a single response. In fact, not a single email from him that entire month.*
>
> *After the month was over, I called him. I took about ten minutes and shared what I was feeling, that I missed him, and how hopeful I was for*

continuing our marriage with a few changes from each of us. I then asked how his month apart went and for his thoughts on our marriage. His response: "It was fine. I didn't really think about our marriage much." He then asked if he should move back in today or wait until after the weekend since he didn't know if I already had plans or not with friends. In that very second I knew my mind was made up, and soon after I filed for divorce. He would never emotionally invest in me, not even at the most crucial moments of our marriage.

I don't know what my future holds, but even though I'm saddened I'm the one who initiated the divorce, I have a sense of peace about it after giving my all.

—Ginny

If you've exhausted all resources and still feel like divorce is the best decision for you, then by all means you've gotta do what you've gotta do. For some of you divorce really is the best option; take Michelle, for example. If this is the case, remember you're not alone and you're going to be just fine. After all, we are the ex-wives, and it's our duty as girlfriends to help you plan and prepare for your journey, but more importantly, to be there to hold your hand throughout this process.

Keep in mind that once you've made the final decision to end your marriage, you're going to feel tremendous guilt. This seems to be a common thread between women who choose to leave, especially if there are kids involved. When doubt starts to settle in, break out your list of reasons why you made the decision to divorce, and keep it close to you. Laminate it if you have to. Listen to your gut and stay true to yourself. Stick to your guns.

#2: Your spouse wants a divorce; you do not

I'm sorry, did you just say you want a divorce? After seventeen years of marriage and all the bullshit I've put up with, the years of forgiveness, the thousands of dollars we've spent in counseling. I've stuck it out, and now you don't want to do this anymore? If anyone was going to walk away it should have been me.

—Chrissi

Your heart is broken, you can't eat or sleep, and your world as you knew it is over. Nothing makes sense. You feel betrayed, shocked, confused, vulnerable, and full of fear. Panic is setting in. Sound familiar? Yes, we've been there.

Your mind is overwhelmed with repeated thoughts such as these:

- What did I do wrong?
- Why does he want to leave?
- Can't we work this out?
- Is there someone else?
- What about the kids?
- How will I survive without him?
- I can't believe this is happening.

The good news: you're going to be okay.

The bad news: it might take a while.

Unfortunately, there isn't an easy fix for a broken heart, but we do have some tips on how you can get through this. There are some important things you need to keep in mind as you journey down this bumpy road.

As desperate as you are to save things and get your life back to normal, remember, the only person you can control is you. Your commitment to saving your marriage is a huge factor in how things progress during this time, but you've got to do things right. The last thing you want to do is make mistakes that will push your spouse even farther away. Think of this as a game of chess—your ultimate goal is to checkmate the king (your husband).

We aren't experts, but we have seen quite a few women turn things around.

> *His thought was: the grass was greener on the other side. I knew better. After two months of separation he thought I would be begging him to come back. I wasn't. I focused on our girls and building a life on the hypothetical "just the three of us" instead of four. Even though this was hard and hurt me, because I really loved my husband, I also needed time to sort some issues out.*
>
> *I was angry with him, as well as angry with myself for some of the things that I had swept under the rug because I was so focused on the kids. He then set New Year's Day as the date he would move back in. The date*

passed without him moving back. It crushed me, but I went about my life, like my friends and family urged me to do. I gave him the space he wanted, and I came to realize I also needed [space] in order to give our marriage another try. He eventually moved back, but not right away. Our marriage is stronger because I was committed, not desperate. And, most importantly, he's a better husband and I'm a better wife.

—Elise

The Ex-Wives' Tips:

- Don't beg him to stay. It might sound good in theory, but it really looks pathetic and will push him even farther away.
- Take a good look in the mirror and be honest with yourself. How have you contributed to the problems in your marriage? Have you been critical, nagging, difficult to live with, etc.? If so, you have to stop these behaviors ASAP. Actions speak louder than words, especially now.
- Back off. Don't pressure him into anything he doesn't want to do. Focus on yourself and give him the space he's requesting.
- Don't compromise your personal morals and values—ever. Insist on respect and keep your boundaries tight.
- Get help. If he refuses to go to counseling, go by yourself. If he's willing to give it a shot, find the best marriage and family counselor you can afford and make an appointment now.

Obviously, we are ex-wives, so we're not exactly professionals at saving marriages. We do, however, want to give you hope. Just because divorce papers have been filed, that doesn't mean you'll end up divorced. And just because he's telling you it's over, doesn't mean it really is.

Just keep calm and by all means carry on. It ain't over 'til the fat lady sings, girlfriend.

Now, this isn't to say you should hang out in la-la land (a.k.a. denial) waiting for his return. If he's requesting a divorce, then you need to get your ducks in a row ASAP. Instead of crawling into bed with a box of Thin Mints, get on the phone and hire an attorney, pronto. Start pulling your financial records and keep a tight watch on your bank accounts. You can't afford to be a shrinking violet right now, and although every inch of your body wants to shrivel up and hide, now is the time to do the exact opposite.

Regardless of whether you reconcile or proceed with divorce, we think it's time for a pep talk. And if there's anything the Ex-Wives love, it's a good pep talk.

This is Your First Pep Talk

You are going to be fine. Right now your life sucks, you're scared to death, and you're wondering if you'll ever smile again. Guess what? You will! We are welcoming you with open arms and lots of good advice to help you through this. You are not alone! Surround yourself with people who love you, and only take advice from those you would trade places with. Hire a badass attorney, and keep your big girl panties on. There's a whole new chapter in your life ready to be written. So let's get started. Everything in life happens for a reason, and as Gloria Gaynor says: "I will survive!"

#3: The divorce is mutual—you both want it

> *My ex-husband and I were married for twenty-one years, and the decision to divorce was completely mutual after our children went to college. We are both happily remarried, but even now, after twenty-five years, I have random unexpected moments of sadness when I think of him. When you share a life with someone, those feelings and memories don't just disappear.*
>
> —Elizabeth

Sometimes things just don't work out. We get it. If you find yourself in this situation, consider yourself lucky. Breaking up is never easy, and it's even harder when one person wants out and the other resists. Thankfully, no one is feeling betrayed or shocked. You've weighed the options, probably attended couples counseling, and have mutually decided the marriage is irreparable. The future looks brighter without each other, and neither one of you is happy. Sounds like an easy way out, even though we all know ending a marriage is never easy.

Divorce will shake up your world, even if both of you agree it's the best decision. Sure, you may not have a big legal battle, but don't be caught off guard when feelings of guilt, doubt, disappointment, and sadness set in. No one is immune to this; it comes with the territory.

We've talked to women all over the world about their experiences with divorce; many exposed their raw emotions and feelings. Here's what some of them had to say regarding the end of their marriage.

I knew my marriage was over when . . .

- I drove laps around my neighborhood because I didn't want to go home.
- I felt more alone with him than without him.
- My children begged me to leave.
- I found myself in bed with another man.
- I overheard my best friend tell him she loved him.
- I realized I was the only one fighting for it.

Maybe your marriage isn't over, but maybe it is. Regardless of your circumstances, divorce sucks. Whether you're the one leaving or the one left brokenhearted, you will inevitably experience the stages of grief. Be prepared to grieve the death of your relationship, but hang in there; there's a light at the end of this tunnel.

Before You Jump Overboard

Divorce is serious business. Before you make any final decisions, we feel it's our duty to encourage you to save your marriage. Keep in mind that we are not licensed counselors or experts on saving marriages (obviously). We don't know your personal situation, so we can only speak from our experiences.

We are advocates for healthy, happy, loving relationships. When couples start discussing divorce, they are most likely at their breaking point. No one is feeling loved and/or happy. This isn't a reason to get divorced. This is, however, a good time to seek professional marital counseling (and limit your outdoor voice).

Marriage counselors are in the business of saving marriages, especially the ones that are worth saving. It's their job to help you navigate rough waters. Regardless of how you're feeling toward your spouse (even if you want to strangle him or leave him on a deserted island with killer monkeys), you made vows to each other for a reason, so it's only fair to give it a shot.

If he's open to seeing a counselor, then by all means, girlfriend, take him up on it. If he refuses counseling, then go by yourself. You just never know until you try.

Sometimes a third party is exactly what you need. You know, a safe place, a Switzerland, if you will; a neutral environment where you can hash out the bad and reconnect with the good. In many cases the threat of divorce can bring a couple closer together. After a few sessions you may find yourselves regaining trust and committing to making things work. If finances are a challenge, look to friends, family, or possibly your place of religious worship for help. There are resources available to you, but sometimes it takes doing a little homework to find them.

It's Over (The Fat Lady Has Sung)

You've come to the realization that this is, in fact, really happening. You have exhausted all avenues for a relationship rescue, and you are prepared to move forward with divorce. It's okay. You will survive. It won't be easy, but you are going to get through this. Now, pick up the phone and call your best friend.

> *I was shocked, and still am. My husband wanted a divorce after seventeen years of marriage. Our kids were set in schools and had their bus and neighborhood buddies. I just couldn't understand why now. Why do this to the kids? Why do this to me, your best friend? But I knew my husband, and there was no going back once his mind was made up. And I told him if he went through with this there would be no going back for me. Our divorce was a rude awakening for me; I just didn't know where to start. Thankfully, I had many friends and family waiting to support me, especially when I didn't even know how to support myself.*
>
> —Kerri

No matter what your situation is, and who wants to start the divorce process, as we've said many times throughout this chapter, it's gonna suck—big time suck. But when something sucks, it doesn't last forever.

This may be the end of your fighting, which will lead to a "new and improved" marriage. This may be the end of your marriage, which will lead you to a "new and improved" you. Or this may just be an end to both, in which case let's get down to business—time to prepare for both a "new and improved" you as well as a "new and improved" life.

Preparing for Your Journey

{this is "the big" pep talk}

"Toto, I've a feeling we're not in Kansas anymore."

—Dorothy (from *The Wizard of Oz*)

If you're anything like us, you're now throwing your hands in the air, exclaiming "Now what?" Possibly with some tears or swears (or both) added in. The life you've been living will soon be in your past, you think. Your future has a big ol' question mark on it, you know. Where in the heck are you now? Welcome to your first destination, The Land of Preparation.

Yes, dear readers, this is not only your first stop, but the most important stop of the entire journey through divorce.

Luckily you have the Ex-Wives here to guide you. Considering our priority is to help you arm yourself with information, we are going to help you prepare as if Napoleon himself has risen from the grave and is ready to do battle against you. Any smart girl knows that information + preparation = win, win, even against a Napoleon.

Now comes the fun part. We are going to ask you to ditch a certain piece of your wardrobe, something you might need in the future but definitely not now: your thongs. (Don't throw them away, just tuck them away in a drawer for now.)

It's officially time to put on those big girl panties we keep mentioning.

Because when preparing for the business of a legal divorce, one needs the appropriate armor, and anything that rides up your rear will not cut it.

They may not be pretty, but damn if big girl panties won't help you deal with anything that comes your way. Big girl panties encourage you to remember that the process of getting a legal divorce is not an emotional transaction, it's a business transaction.

Your boundaries will need to be drawn bolder than they ever have been before, as in black permanent, never coming off, marker. Say no and mean absofreakinlutely no way. Say yes and mean hell yes. Say, "Let me think about that," the majority of times, and actually breathe and think about it, without the pressure of time limitations. Don't cave in if you're being pressured. Absolutely no big decisions should be made without careful thought and review. Get where we're going here?

Bullying is not allowed on our playgrounds anymore. It's time to get on your feet and stand up for your fabulous future self. Your decisions and actions during the process of divorce will affect almost every aspect of your future life. So buy an entire new wardrobe of BGPs—you're gonna need them.

The Business of Divorce vs. Personal Divorce

business [**biz**-nis]: that with which a person is principally and seriously concerned

personal [**pur**-suh-nl]: of, relating to, or coming as from a particular person; individual; private

As ex-wives, we know that this is going to be a very emotional time of your life, and it will be hard to separate the emotional part of divorce from the business side of divorce. But this is the one time you must truly separate business (legal divorce) from personal (private, sobbing, nonstop eating an entire freezer's worth of Ben and Jerry's Hazed & Confused, while tearing up photos of your soon-to-be ex).

Let us say this, and let it sear into your big, beautiful brain: you must take care of yourself emotionally in order to do business like the mogul we know you are (we'll go into that more soon). Ask yourself if you would work for a boss that went on emotional tirades, sobbed uncontrollably at the most inopportune times, or didn't have their s@#t together? You wouldn't.

You, soon-to-be ex-wife, get to be the CEO of your divorce! That's right, Chief Empress Organizer of your divorce. The BIG BOSS!

So, order the desk nameplate, or print off those business cards you've been eyeing on Pear Tree even though you're a stay-at-home mom, because it's up to you to run this business of divorce you are about to enter into. More importantly, it's up to you to set the tone for a divorce that's as pain free as possible.

What kind of boss do you want to be? You want to be the boss everyone thinks has their life so freaking together because they are so überorganized that they probably have all of their freshly ironed clothing on wooden hangers facing the same direction, sorted by color and sleeve length, in their custom-built mahogany walk-in closet. That's how together we want your soon-to-be ex to think you are. (Even if you're shoveling in pints of ice cream while defacing wedding pictures on top of piles of dirty, crumpled clothing on the floor of a closet that's barely big enough to hold a broom.)

Leave the emotion, as well as the drama, out of your role as CEO in your business of divorce. Take it from us: your financial, custodial, and future kickass self is going to depend on this.

Time to earn your new title of Empress and focus on the most essential piece, organization.

Organizing

So, what exactly will you be organizing to help you get to your happy, shiny new life after divorce? Just about everything. Every professional you hire or encounter—attorney, county clerk, counselor, mediator, child psychologist, financial planner, post-divorce party planner (okay, maybe not her)—will need documents from you. Not just a couple, but many documents.

Be prepared to whisper sweet nothings to a copier or scanner and spend a day or so collecting/sifting/sorting/scouring your paperwork to find everything you need and get organized. We want you to bolt straight out of the gate, not wobble out wearily as we did. Hire a babysitter, ask your most OCD friends to help you for an afternoon, or do whatever you have to do to get ready to create binders and folders even Martha Stewart would approve of. Trust us, the work and organization you do now in the initial stages of your divorce is what will get you to the finish line without collapsing from mental exhaustion.

Suggested First Steps for Organization of Financial Matters:

1. Change all passwords, as in ALL passwords that would potentially give your soon-to-be ex access to any private information. And, yes, that includes your Delta SkyMiles account.
2. Order or request credit reports from all three reporting bureaus and put a freeze on your credit. This way no one will be able to apply for credit under your name without the lending institution contacting you first for approval.
3. Open a new checking and/or savings account with you as the sole name on the account.
4. Open a new credit card in your name only.
5. Rent a post-office box where you can start receiving personal and/or financial mail.
6. Start saving money or filtering some into your new account for emergency purposes or rainy days (light showers or monsoons). We can't tell you how many women exclaimed that they were shocked when their ex withdrew all of the money from their joint checking account.
7. Be smart and start stocking up on what you might need later for rainy days; gift cards, credits, and vouchers.
8. Start having your paychecks or any earned income deposited directly into your new accounts. Only transfer what is needed to pay joint expenses into the joint accounts if you and your soon-to-be ex decide to keep them open for now.
9. Make sure you retain and make duplicates of each and every account you have that is a liquid asset.
10. Make a list of every tangible asset you possess individually and jointly. Sometimes things tend to go "missing," so if you have a picture as well as notes it's amazing how quickly things can be "found."

11. Speak candidly to your financial planner or accountant about the impending divorce and ask for suggestions on protecting your financial future.
12. Start asking your friends and people you respect for attorney referrals. The faster you call and schedule initial consultations, the quicker you'll know what your personal situation most likely entails.

As we discuss at length in Chapter 5, "Get Organized, Girl," every document or bit of information you can gather will save you money, lots of money. And smart girls don't waste money.

Not only will it save you money, but it will also give you a quick reference tool when you're asked the same questions over and over, which, in turn, will save your sanity. And if there's one thing the Ex-Wives learned the hard way, it's that you can't put a price tag on sanity.

Suggested First Steps for Organization of Personal Matters

1. Make a list of your "must haves" versus "would like to haves" versus "don't care" when it comes to your divorce. Be honest about this and be realistic. "Must haves" are deal breakers, and you don't want to waste those on something trivial. Save them for the times when you want to draw the line in the proverbial sand.
2. Speak to a personal counselor via your church, synagogue, community, paid professional, etc. Schedule a visit and get on it. There's no avoiding going through the seven stages of grief, and they are not pretty without the help of respected, experienced, and trusted individuals.
3. Remember the golden rule: What you put out into the universe returns to you. If you spend your days bad-mouthing your soon-to-be ex to everyone and anyone, or have a one-way ticket on the negative train daily, stop it now. It will only end up hurting you.
4. Map out, collage, or journal what you envision your future life will look like until you've run out of glue or ink (or both). Put your vision somewhere you will see it (Valerie's is in her closet, and Holiday keeps hers on the mirror in her bathroom) to remind you daily that you have everything you need to be everything you want.

5. Be honest with family and friends about your relationship status (no, that doesn't mean plastering sassy crap all over Facebook), but keep the "ace card" up your sleeve. Realize that even though your family and friends love and support you, their advice, actions, and opinions are going to be based on their personal experiences as well as their relationship with your soon-to-be ex, not yours. This is a big change for everyone. Try not to take things personally when you get unexpected, unsolicited advice, or when they still communicate with your ex. Keep those big girl panties hiked high, ladies.
6. Keep a daily calendar of how much time your soon-to-be ex is spending with your children, as well as any information that would be pertinent to giving the best day-to-day chronicle of your family life. This will be your saving grace if it becomes a bigger battle than you think it will be, because 75 percent of the time it does.

Additionally, you will need to start taking copious notes on just about everything. Think communication, daily expenses, household expenses, behaviors, etc. To get you headed down the right path of super-duper A+ note-taking, you'll find worksheets at the back of the book, as well as online at www.exwivesguide.com.

Besides being the best damn CEO of divorce there ever was, the more notes you take, the more organized you will be during future meetings with individuals you are forking money over to. The more organized you are, the more you will be able to save money and your sanity as well as not stray from your "must haves" (a.k.a. more visitation time with the kiddos, not a meaningless velvet Elvis).

Because if we know anything, it's this: a woman who is unorganized or in disarray feels it in every fiber of her being and literally and figuratively becomes a mess!

Emotions and Personal Divorce

To ensure a successful business divorce, clichéd or not, you must "save the drama for your mama." Or save it for your girlfriends, or therapist, or voodoo doll—whoever will give you fifteen minutes to vent/stress/freak the hell out. It's defined as "private" for a reason.

That doesn't mean you have to try to force those spewing feelings back where they came from. We are in no way telling you to pretend like you're not also having a personal divorce. Create time and space in constructive capacities to let the lavalike emotions ooze out slowly in order to keep you from erupting.

How does one constructively do this? This is the perfect time for you to take up that sport or hobby you have put off for years. Valerie always wanted to play tennis but never felt she had the time or energy. Let's just say once she uttered, "I'm not okay with what happened, and I'm not sure I want to be married anymore (insert bad word here)," during her third divorce, she picked up a tennis racket and hasn't put it down since. Hitting balls as hard as she could gave her the opportunity to beat up on something, as opposed to someone, like she was dreaming of doing.

Joining teams provided her the chance to meet new people and increased her support system. Playing in weekend matches gave her something constructive to do when her little one was with her ex and all she wanted to do was watch the Lifetime network all weekend and eat an entire jumbo-size bag of Twizzlers.

You get the drift. Want to get your om on? Take up yoga. Do you always look at runners and think, *Why the hell are they so happy*? Try running and find out. Been dying to travel but your soon-to-be ex hated it so the farthest you traveled was your county line? Update your passport and go see the world, or get out locally for day trips that are budget friendly to feel connected to what both your heart and soul are pulling you toward.

> *My ex hardly ever supported or encouraged the fact that I played a musical instrument. I started having children shortly after marriage, so I never felt like I had the time to do the things I enjoyed. Once we started the divorce, a friend that knew I used to play an instrument invited me to go to a community band practice with her. She thought it would be good for me to do something for myself, even if it was for only two hours a week, and to get my mind off the intensity of my divorce. Boy, was she right. Not only did playing again bring something I loved back into my life, both during and well after my divorce, but it's also how I eventually met my second husband, who is also a musician.*
>
> —Chris

We also suggest drawing a map of what the "new and improved" you looks like, which we touched on briefly in the Organization section. We both collaged what our ideal life would look like after divorce. It was bright, full of boundaries, and had us spreading joy just about anywhere the sun shined, especially while wearing outfits from the pages of the Anthropologie Lookbook. Remember, this is your second chance; don't blow it by not envisioning it.

Women by nature are visual creatures; if we see it, we can achieve it. It's also important for you to set up safety nets anywhere you predict you will most likely fall. If you know you can't handle seeing your soon-to-be ex without sobbing or screaming (or both), it's best to make sure anytime he picks up the kiddos it's at someone else's home, or school, or aftercare.

No kids? Well, then any time you have to meet your soon-to-be ex meet him somewhere public, where going postal would be a no-no. Think Barnes & Noble café—inside voice mandatory and it's usually pretty crowded, total lifesaver.

Hate being by yourself? Schedule your weekends at least a few weeks in advance. Make plans with your friends, visit local exhibits, and attend community social events so you always have something that keeps you connected to others. You know those single gal pals who keep you out until 2:00 a.m. and then you wake up with a fast-food bag mysteriously on your nightstand? Plan to meet them for a quick happy hour right after work or an alcohol-free brunch instead, so you don't end up doing something you know you (and your waistline) will regret.

Most importantly, plan on being emotional, going through the seven stages of grief, and having to carve out and envision a new life for yourself. Even the most amicable of divorces is a major change for you. It's also a huge change for your family and your day-to-day routine. This brings us to the next most important thing you can prepare for as you embark on your journey through divorce . . . your expectations.

Be Realistic

Reality—not always our friend, but not always our foe. Not being realistic with the changes that will and are happening is normally what takes the wind out of our sails or steers even the most vigilant of us on the wrong course.

Take charge early on to set the tone for **accepting and preparing for change, not fighting it.** And as we all know from Oprah, change starts with ourselves, lovely ladies. Plan for the worst and expect the best. That way you won't ever be more than halfway disappointed but might actually be pleasantly surprised.

Strategies based on reality—Create a strategy based on everything you know for sure, have organized, or discovered so far. Facts speak for themselves. Don't have just one strategy; have several plans of action. You never know how somebody is going to act or react to your best-laid plans, especially a soon-to-be ex.

Don't make rash decisions based on feelings. Prioritize, research, organize, look at the facts and truly analyze them from every angle (just like the talented CEO we know you are). Then, write down a couple of possible outcomes in pencil. As smart women, we know changes, and more changes, may happen during our divorces. This is reality, and we need to accept that. Spend this time anticipating any potential pitfalls that might happen so if they do you're already a step ahead.

Time to be savers, not spenders—Step away from the Target cart. Yes, sadly you read that correctly, and luckily it wasn't being shouted to you over the loudspeaker at Target. It's part of preparing for your divorce journey. Put back the chic new lamp, fab new spring door wreath, and the ten other shiny, pretty items you don't really need. The reality is, only a very, very, (did we say *very* yet?) few of us get to maintain our previous lifestyles. We promise your glorious days of filling up the bright red cart will come again, but not for a while. Better to have that extra money in your bank account than to be worried whether you'll eventually have to live out of a shopping cart. So, seriously, you in the home goods section, put it back now.

Be smart, rather than emotional, with your money. This is no time to buy the Hunter boots you've been eyeing forever because you need a pick-me-up as you prepare for divorce. However, it is the time to stock up on Publix gift cards every time you buy groceries (this goes mostly unnoticed; we ex-wives can vouch for this). You never know if you'll find yourself strapped in the future, and at least you know your children will be fed if you have grocery store gift cards. Because if the bottom falls out, nobody in the soup kitchen line is going to say, "Great Hunter boots!"

Valerie assumed because of her third ex's choices and behaviors during their marriage that their divorce was going to be calm and straightforward, with her firmly holding the reins. She asked for the moon and the stars, oh, and the planet and the galaxies, too. Valerie expected to get everything because things had been civil, and she had supported her ex in bettering himself at a time most others wouldn't have. Guess what? Her ex grew a set the day he moved out. He made it his mission to fight for the aforementioned moon and stars (and the planet and galaxies) all while wielding ninja knives and a Freddy Krueger mask. Had Valerie been realistic, she probably wouldn't have suffered the catastrophic financial loss, as well as the emotional torture that seemed never-ending during and after the divorce.

The more organized and realistic you are about what the next several months or years may hold, the sooner you'll be able to ditch the big girl panties and put your thong back on. And if that's not an incentive, we don't know what is.

Stages of Divorce

{*brace yourself*}

"Grief is in two parts. The first is loss. The second is the remaking of life."

—Anne Roiphe

Michael and I were high school sweethearts. We married shortly after college, built a dream house in our small hometown, and spent weekends with friends. Many thought we had a perfect marriage, including me. Everything changed the night I found him in my best friend's tent during our annual summer camping trip. They told me they loved each other and were planning to marry. My world instantly collapsed. He was the only man I had ever loved, and she was more like a sister than a friend. I stood there, in the middle of a campground, completely shocked. I had been betrayed by the two people closest to me.

—Denise

You can google a lot of things, but a cure for heartbreak isn't one of them. Truth be told, there isn't an easy way to get through the mess of divorce. Divorce is the death of a relationship, but more importantly, it's the death of a dream. The dream of a happily ever after, the dream of the "perfect" family (believe us, there is no such thing), and the dream of sharing forever with your spouse. The whole "till death do us part" thing has gone flying out the window, and you're just trying to figure out how to make it through the day without another massive crying session.

Don't give up just yet. A slew of shrinks have done their research, and according to the experts there's a specific cycle of grief you can expect to experience. Seeing how knowledge is, in fact, power, we thought it would be helpful to share these stages with you. And remember, as we will remind you over and over, this too shall pass.

Thanks to Elisabeth Kübler-Ross (author of *On Death and Dying*, 1969), we can identify the five stages of grief as follows:

1. Denial
2. Anger
3. Bargaining
4. Depression
5. Acceptance

Sorry, girlfriend, there isn't a magic button that can fast-forward you to acceptance, but we seriously believe that if you process and acknowledge each stage, you'll find yourself accepting your situation much quicker than if you stick your head in a pillow and ignore what's really happening. Hint: if your head is stuck in a pillow, you're currently in denial.

While acceptance is the ultimate goal, keep in mind that the process of grief isn't linear. You won't move seamlessly from one stage to the next. (Although that would certainly make things a little easier—wish there was a suggestion box for that one!) The feelings of grief are better illustrated as a chaotic circle, similar to the Mad Tea Party ride at Disney World. Constant pushing, pulling, and twisting in multiple directions interfere with your ability to focus, leaving you dizzy and nauseous. We can't help but wonder why there's always a crazy long line for this ride. Using your Fast Pass for this ride . . . total insanity, but we wish. In all seriousness, our best advice would be to hold on tight and remember that eventually the ride will end. Of course, some rides will be longer than others, but one day you'll step out of your teacup, the dizziness will fade, and your focus will change.

While we can't predict exactly what will happen or how you will feel during these stages, we can share our personal experiences and the lessons we learned. Personal circumstances also significantly contribute to how you react during each stage of grief. If you were blindsided by your husband's request for divorce, your process of grief is going to be different from the woman who has finally mustered the strength to leave an abusive marriage.

Thanks to years of research we can identify these stages of grief, and while we may not go through them in exactly the same way, you can expect to find yourself somewhere on the spectrum on any given day.

Stage 1: DENIAL

This is just a bad dream

Our bodies are pretty amazing. In fact, we have this incredible ability to protect our minds (and hearts) from pain and shock. This coping mechanism is called denial, and for some it's a favorable stage in the grieving process. After all, there's much to be said about putting on a brave face and pretending everything is going to be A-OK. "This isn't really happening," or "I'm sure he'll change his mind, it's just a phase," are examples of signs that you're in denial. Denial is like the calm before the storm; you know, that peaceful, yet eerie, blanket of silence that prefaces a hurricane. Yep, that silence would be denial, and the hurricane is blowing loudly and rapidly behind it ready to rip your roof off.

If you're the one who's chosen to leave the marriage, your denial stage may have come prior to your request for divorce. Most likely there have been days, months, or even years leading up to your decision to end the marriage. Thoughts such as "Things will get better," or "My life could be much worse," or "He promised he would change," are just a few examples. Denial can also be the culprit of abusive relationships, and maybe it was these very feelings of denial that caused you to stay married longer than you should have.

If you're in denial, please listen carefully. This is not the time to make any major promises, such as signing legal documents or agreeing to final custody terms. Get your head out of the pillow before you sign on the dotted line. You're vulnerable, weak, and not thinking clearly.

Rushing through the denial process is kind of, well, impossible. (Again, we tried it.) You can't force your heart to face the truth; this is a mental thing. Once your brain catches on, you'll swiftly realize what's about to happen. Instead of being broken and confused, that beautiful poetic heart of yours is going to get mad.

Stage 2: ANGER

Are you f#$% kidding me?*

Reality has set in and you're pissed, really, really pissed. Go ahead, let it out. This isn't the time to be polite or ladylike. It's kind of like having an emotional "get out of jail free" card, but not really, so please don't do anything illegal. The calm before the storm is over, and the hurricane is in full swell, tearing down everything and anything in its path. Think Godzilla stomping through the eye of the hurricane and that should paint an accurate enough picture.

During the anger phase your ex will become the enemy. Instead of romanticizing the past, you'll remember everything about this man that pissed you off. Whether it was his sloppy habit of leaving facial hair in the sink, lack of finesse in the bedroom, hotheaded temper, clipping his toenails in bed, smoking, horrible money management, little man syndrome, heavy breathing, loud chewing—you get where we're going here—he will quickly become incredibly undesirable in your eyes. This is a good thing, roll with it!

Suggestion: write these down for future reference. This list will come in handy when depression kicks in and you start feeling lonely.

Believe it or not, this can be a healthy stage. Your heart recognizes the pain it's feeling and lashes out accordingly. Anger is also a sign that you're beginning to move on. Everything was tucked in nice and neat during denial, but now the caged lion is breaking free and has meat on the brain. We say let 'er rip, girlfriend (as long as little ears can't hear you). You've earned the right to that mighty roar.

The Ex-Wives' Dos and Don'ts of Anger:

- DO allow yourself to feel angry.
- DON'T do anything you could potentially regret (like attacking him with the pepper spray he gave you for Christmas last year—unless, of course, it's self-defense ☺).
- DO share your feelings with people you trust: close family, friends, or a professional counselor/therapist.
- DON'T drag your children into your feelings of anger. Keep those mama bear instincts intact and protect your kids.

Anger came pretty quickly for me. One night during dinner my husband announced he was in love with his secretary and moving out the next weekend. Denial lasted for about thirty seconds, and after that I just wanted to kill him.

—Kimberly

Stage 3: BARGAINING

But I'll do anything . . .

This stage is tricky. You're at a major fork in the road, and as far as you're concerned all you have to do is get back on the marriage trail and things will be just fine. You've gone through denial, you've been angry and upset, and now you're starting to feel the need to regain control. Bargaining is a last-ditch effort to get your life, your marriage, your normal back.

If you're the one who left the marriage, this is when you'll realize that you have either

a) made the right decision

or

b) made a huge mistake

Hint: If you think you've made a huge mistake, we strongly recommend you RUN, not walk, home.

If your spouse was the one to leave, bargaining is where you will do anything and everything to win him back. The feelings you're experiencing now are tough, and the obvious solution is to fix the problem and attempt to repair the damage that has been done as opposed to face the uncertain. "I know our life wasn't perfect, but I just can't handle this . . . I'll do whatever it takes."

This can be an ugly process, involving groveling, begging, pleading, reasoning, and even bribing. While we strongly advise against the use of these tactics, we realize you're probably not going to listen. Remember, your spouse will also experience the bargaining stage, and if he believes he's made a mistake, eventually he will come back to you. (Sometimes this takes longer than we would like, but hold tight. You never know, and it normally involves an apology with a flashy, blingy sort of thing.)

When my husband filed for divorce, I felt completely helpless. I was lonely, angry, and confused. I would have done anything to win him back. I sacrificed my self-worth by offering forgiveness for years of infidelity, was willing to repay the thousands of dollars of debt he racked up, and even promised him guilt-free weekends to play golf if he would just come home. I didn't care what I had to do or what indiscretions I needed to forget. I just wanted my life, and my husband, back. My bargaining didn't work, and although it was the most painful time of my life, I am so thankful he didn't buy into my pleas. He never treated me with the respect or love I deserved, but it took me several years to realize that.

—Julie

The Ex-Wives' Advice:

Hold your head up high and surround yourself with people who love you. They will help you maintain your dignity, or at least throw a bucket of water in your face to wake you up if you start to slip.

Stage 4: DEPRESSION

This sucks

We're not going to sugarcoat this for you. Divorce sucks. It really, really, really sucks, and the depression stage is probably the worst. Keep in mind, you're probably going to cycle in between different stages at various times, just be prepared for the feeling of depression to set in.

Don't be surprised if depression creeps up on you. It's kind of like an unwanted houseguest. You have no idea when it's going to knock on your door, but when it does, it takes over. Your fancy soaps will lose their luster, meals no longer have the same appeal, and hiding in your bedroom makes you feel both better and guilty. And you never know when the unwanted houseguest will leave, no matter how hard you try to get it to pack up and just go home.

Depression is tough to control. In fact, most of us experience depression along with whatever other stage we're currently processing. The feelings of sadness, loneliness, and lack of motivation can send you into a dark spiral at any given moment.

I'll never forget the time I was checking out at the grocery store and our wedding song came on in the background. Tears streamed down my face, and I couldn't control the sadness. It hit me like a Mack truck.

—Megan

I realized I was depressed when I found myself eating Raisin Bran out of a coffee mug in bed for the fourth day in a row. In my mind I had no reason to get dressed or leave the house. I was in survival mode, and depression had definitely kicked in.

—Jennifer

One week I literally didn't leave my house for three straight days. Not even to get the mail. I just ate, watched TV, and slept on the sofa the entire time. It wasn't until day four that I realized I hadn't changed out of my clothes either. A friend stopped by to see if I was okay, and I pretended I had a stomach bug so she couldn't come in. Not changing clothes and piling up empty bottles of Gatorade on my family room table is one thing, but not wanting to see one of my good friends? Yes, I had finally hit depression, and I didn't even have the energy to care.

—Valerie

While it's perfectly acceptable to skip a shower here or there, don't fall into the trap of wallowing in self-pity for more than a few days. Now is the time to seek professional help from a divorce counselor or marriage and family therapist. We know you think your situation is unique, but truth be told, these pros have seen it all. Chances are your story is very similar to ours.

The Ex-Wives' Advice:

Everyone handles depression differently. Some people retreat and completely isolate themselves. Others respond by booking their social calendars to the gills, not leaving any room for time alone or, even worse, silence.

Divorce is kind of a textbook operation; there are certain things that typically happen while going through the process, and depression just happens to be one of them.

Instead of tackling your demons alone, we strongly recommend you confide in close family members and friends and seek professional help. You might think you've got it under control, but, girlfriend, a week (or more) in bed without basic personal hygiene is a flashing neon sign that you're in need of an intervention. Ditch the sweatpants, break out your favorite sugar scrub, and hit the shower, or better yet, the day spa if you followed our earlier advice and tucked away money for a "rainy day." Hitting the depression stage certainly counts as one to us!

> *I will never forget the first time my children left my home to spend the weekend with their dad. The minute I closed the door behind them I fell to the floor in tears. I realized there was no denying the pain of my current truth. I think it was the silence that hurt the most. It was unbearable . . . the emptiness, loneliness, and overall feeling of helplessness. The thought of staying in the silent, empty house alone just broke my heart. I grabbed my keys and left. I didn't know where I was going, but I knew I had to go somewhere.*
>
> —Holiday

Stage 5: ACCEPTANCE

On the bright side

You've been through the wringer, your heart has started to heal, and believe it or not, there's a flicker of light at the end of the tunnel. Welcome to acceptance, girlfriend! While this stage doesn't mean you won't feel the pain of loss or sadness, you're starting to get your groove back. Rock on and don't look back!

Acceptance is an absolute cakewalk compared to the other stages of grief. Remember the Mad Tea Party ride? You've now stepped out of the cup and onto solid ground. As promised, the dizziness is fading, and you're regaining focus. Looking back, the tears, fits of rage, and brief moments of insanity seem like a total waste of time. You're ready to take the next step and embrace a new life.

*__Warning:__ Depression has a sneaky way of creeping in during all stages of grief, including this one.

Give yourself permission to have authentic feelings, but don't allow them to paralyze you. Keep moving forward.

The most important thing to remember during this process is just that: it's a process. Unlike a trip to the grocery store, you can't just breeze down the aisle and check things off a list. Divorce doesn't work like that. We're confident you will progress through recovery; be patient with yourself and allow your heart the time it needs to heal.

CAUTION:

Divorce, like the death of a loved one, results in grief. While we can pretty much guarantee you'll experience all five stages of emotional grief, they could occur in any order. Chances are you'll repeat the cycle multiple times . . . just hang on for the ride and do your best to get through the rough patches. Acceptance and hope are just around the corner.

The Ex-Wives' Advice:

- Allow yourself to grieve and thoroughly experience each stage of the process. There's no beginning, middle, or end to these stages. You will most likely experience them several times; remember, it's a circular process.
- REST. Grief takes a toll on your body. You need to rest and allow your body (and heart) to heal.
- Connect with people and get out of the house. Don't alienate yourself.
- Give yourself a three-day sweatpants/elastic waist rule. Sorry, we're not budging on this one.
- Keep a gratitude journal. Be thankful and have a heart of gratitude. We know it's hard, but the more you practice the attitude of gratitude, the easier it will get, we promise.
- Channel your inner Oprah and take note of your favorite things. Finding joy in the little things can be helpful during this process.
- Participate in activities that you enjoy and do things that make YOU happy (hobbies, sports, etc.).
- Don't take advice from anyone you wouldn't trade places with, period. Ignore any horror stories you may hear; everyone's divorce is different, especially if it's someone from a different generation.

Get Organized, Girl

{let's talk money, honey}

"Organization is what you do before you do something, so that when you do it, it is not all mixed up."

—A. A. Milne

Divorce, quite simply put, is a business transaction, as we touched on in the third chapter, "Preparing for Your Journey." Even though by definition divorce is the legal dissolution of a marriage by the courts, it also involves dividing almost everything you jointly acquired during the marriage, and I do mean almost everything. So put down the Kleenex (and the third box of Thin Mint cookies you have eaten in the last twenty-four hours) and start thinking like a man.

Not only will you be figuring out how to divide assets like 401(k)s and deciding who's responsible for which joint debt, you will also be figuring out who gets awarded said assets. Yep, that includes the brand-new Pottery Barn sofa you had your eyes on for years and finally purchased six months before the you-know-what really hit the fan. Do we have your attention now?

Do yourself the biggest favor you can and take the emotion out of divorce when it comes to gathering the many financial documents that will be required. Your present and future financial security depend on it.

Both the attorneys and the courts are going to require you to gather several financial documents. This is of the utmost importance, and the more work you do on providing everything, the better chance you have of having a favorable outcome.

Additionally, the more effort you put into compiling all of the required documents yourself, the more money you will save. Whether you're participating in discovery or preparing it yourself, if attorneys need to get involved (something extreme, such as having to subpoena records, or as simple as calling or emailing you to discuss missing documents) you will be charged for it. And we all know smart girls would rather spend the extra hours getting the documents they need as opposed to wasting money on needless attorney's fees.

That goes for your soon-to-be ex also. Generally speaking, men may not understand joint cooperation when they're angry or upset, but they do understand money.

It would be wise to thoroughly discuss with your soon-to-be ex the importance of providing and compiling all needed paperwork when it comes to financial aspects. It will actually help keep money in both of your accounts (yes, his too), which in turn will give you more to divide. Win-win!

So now you're thinking, *OK, I definitely want to be awarded the Pottery Barn sofa, and I don't want to have to pay my attorney two thousand-plus dollars (and my ex pays his attorney the same if not more) to get hold of documents we both could have provided. I will put on my best "I mean business" outfit and discuss this with my soon-to-be ex in a calm, businesslike manner. Besides, that's money we could spend on other areas of our life that are a little more important once we move on as singletons, such as our child, or somewhere to live, or the matching Pottery Barn loveseat I really wanted to go with the sofa.*

So, let's break this down into steps:

Step 1. Purchase/Gather the Following:

1. Two large accordion file folders
2. Thirty to fifty manila or colored file folders
3. Highlighters
4. Printer ink (you will be printing/copying a TON of papers)
5. Two reams of paper
6. Pen and notebook

Once you have all of these items together, go ahead and get ready to spread out wherever you keep the majority of your documents. Turn on your favorite tunes, pour a glass of wine (we said a glass, not a bottle), and get ready to channel your inner admin. Now boot up the computer and turn on the printer, because you are about to kill a tree.

Step 2. Start Collecting, Printing, and Copying Documents

Typically, you will need to provide a minimum of twelve months' worth of all statements, further back throughout the course of the marriage if any unusual or uncharacteristic activity has taken place. Whether you receive printed statements in the mail or e-statements online, you will need to access each of these accounts.

It is imperative for you to have all of the logins, passwords, pass keys, telephone codes, verbal passwords, secret knocks, and so on documented. This would be the perfect time to write each one down as you access each account.

Use our handy "Accounts" worksheet, found in the Resources section of this book as well as online at www.exwivesguide.com, and write down the name of every service provider or institution you have an account with, as well as the phone number, email address, and login/password credentials. Triple laminate this sheet. Not only will laminating it make you realize what a go-to resource it will be during your divorce, but it will also shield it from any wine spills. (Notice I didn't say *tears* here, since we are in business mode, right?) As many of you know, divorce does not happen in the blink of an eye. Most divorces take anywhere from ninety days to two years to finalize. So you will probably have to update these statements every few months. Having all of this information in one place is key, as it will save you hours later.

Here is a list of documents and statements you will need to compile and make a minimum of two copies of:

Utilities

- Gas/oil bills
- Electric bills
- Water bills

- Cable bills
- Internet bills
- Landline and wireless phone bills

Revolving and Installment

- Credit cards (joint, personal, and business if applicable)
- Mortgage statements
- Home equity line of credit statements
- Lease (if you are renting)
- Last two years of property and vehicle tax bills
- Secured loans
- Unsecured loans
- Family loans
- Automobile loans
- Medical bills
- Other fixed payments

Financial

- Checking account statements
- Savings account statements
- Investment account statements
- Retirement account statements (401(k), IRA, etc.)
- Stocks and bonds
- Annuities
- Mutual funds statements
- 529 college savings plan statements
- Medical savings account statements
- Children's savings account statements
- Copy of any trusts
- Amount of cash on hand

Employment/Income/Self-Employed Business

- Pay stubs for the past sixty days
- The past two to five years of filed tax returns (personal, joint, business)
- Past two years; bonus or commission statements

- Additional perks/benefits (car allowance, etc.)
- Business expenses (reimbursed and non-reimbursed)
- Accounts receivable
- Accounts payable
- Profit and loss statement for the past six months
- Twelve months of business bank statements (more if deemed necessary)
- Existing contracts
- Stock options

Personal

- Birth certificates
- Social security cards for every family member
- Passports for every family member
- Driver's licenses for every family member
- Marriage license (we're hoping you haven't burned it quite yet)
- Life insurance policies
- Will
- Health, dental, and vision insurance cards

Deeds/Titles

- Car titles
- Boat, RV, etc. titles
- Deed to home
- Deed to other properties or land owned

Appraised Assets

- Jewelry appraisals
- Artwork appraisals
- Collection appraisals
- Appraisals of other high-value items

Miscellaneous

- Gym memberships
- Club memberships (country club, Costco, Bon Jovi fan club)

- Season tickets
- Organization memberships (museums, zoo, etc.)
- Frequent flyer miles
- Gift certificates
- Loyalty memberships (hotels, rental cars, DSW shoes, etc.)

I couldn't believe how expensive getting divorced was. If I knew then what I know now, I would have acted sooner on putting aside some of our joint money and being a little bit more of a DIY girl when it came to gathering information and making copies. The very first month I got my attorney's invoice I opened it and just looked at the bottom line figure. After two months in, I decided to really start looking at the breakdown of fees and hours, since it was getting so costly. I almost fell over when I saw I had been billed for four hours of work at $250 an hour to make copies and "reorganize" my file my first month, on top of the many other charges. And the worst part was, I wasn't surprised; what I turned in was incomplete and a mess. I had wasted one thousand dollars on something I could have easily done myself. A few weeks after that charge I had to hold off on registering my son for baseball because it was one hundred and sixty-five dollars and I didn't have it. I should have looked at the details on the very first bill!

—Hillary

Step 3: Separating Your Documents

Now that smoke is pouring out of your printer or copier from overuse, it's time to make use of the handy-dandy supplies we suggested you have in Step 1.

Make sure that you have separated each of the above items into individual piles. After you have done that, start labeling your file folders accordingly. This would be a great time for all of you aspiring Martha Stewarts to color-code the eight categories for easy retrieval.

One of your two copies can go in one large pile to give to your attorney; the rest should have files labeled and created for them. You don't really need to label those individually for your attorney unless you are really on a roll or bought the one thousand-count box of file folders at Costco and are on a mission to see if you can use them all.

Anything in the first four categories—Utilities, Revolving and Installment, Financial, Employment/Income/Self-Employed Business—will go into a separate file for each account.

For example:

Utilities—Gas	Utilities—Water
Revolving—My AmEx	Revolving—Our Discover Card
Installment—My Car	Installment—Our SunTrust Loan
Financial—My Ivy Funds	Financial—His 401(k)
Income—His Pay Stubs	Business—My Profit & Loss

For the last four categories—Personal, Deeds/Titles, Appraised Assets, Miscellaneous—label a single file with each of the category titles. All of the items listed under the category can go into one file. If you really want to break them out, go for it. However, these are items you won't need to access as much. Once you have a copy of these it's unlikely you'll need to update them.

For example:

Personal—Inside are the driver's licenses, passports, marriage certificate (slightly charred), and so on.

Step 4: Organize Your File Folders

Now you'll put those two large, expandable, accordion-style file holders to use. One you will use to house all of the file folders you made from the first four categories. If you have an exceedingly large number of these files, then purchase another accordion file holder, but remember to keep all the files in the same category together.

The second file holder will be used for everything from the last four categories. You won't want to bring this file holder back and forth to your attorney's office, as it contains items that are not easily replaced.

Lose a copy of a utility bill, no problem. Lose a copy of your social security card, big problem.

Once you have your file folders nicely stored for easy access and quick transport, you should have the rather large pile of second copies you made of everything. Put these copies in an envelope, file folder, or whatever you prefer (or what they will fit in).

> *The first two times I got divorced all (and I do mean all) my documents fit neatly in an average-size envelope. For my third divorce I needed about four XXX-large envelopes and binders, as well as a forklift to carry them.*
>
> —Valerie

Step 5: Developing a Workable Budget

All your statements and documents have now been printed, copied, and sorted. So what's next, run the world? Well, almost. In order to run the world you need to have a budget. (Many politicians have tried to do this without one . . . need we say more?) Without a budget your world will most likely be one of chaos and confusion, and we all know how that plays out on the highlight reel on CNN. It's no different for you.

Some of you might be thinking, *Well, I'm not really sure how much child support, alimony, or blood out of a turnip I am either going to squeeze, receive, or be responsible for paying. So how can I develop an accurate budget?*

Our response: figure out a way to **never** rely solely on that money from your soon-to-be ex for your budget, or your new life. We know this may seem impossible at first, especially for those of us who weren't working full time prior to the divorce. But we promise it's doable; we ex-wives are living proof.

Making a two-year plan to secure your own financial destiny is highly recommended. If you bought this book, we know you're bright. So go share your talents with the world; make that money, honey. Be an example and show others that when the phoenix does rise, it soars even higher!

Don't know where to start to create a budget? You will find worksheets for proposed expenses and income in the Resources section in the back of the book and online at www.exwivesguide.com. You should now be able to fill in the blanks, due to the fact that you did a phenomenal job of collecting all the information. We warn you, it will most likely change by the time you go to mediation, court, or finalize your divorce, but at least you will be able to see what the initial financial picture should look like.

> *My husband and I had a pretty amiable divorce, and we decided to use an independent mediation counselor to help us come to financial conclusions in order to save money with our attorneys. We both had to spend the many hours it takes to collect financial documents. The bottom line wasn't nearly as bad as I thought it would be; however, it wasn't quite what I was hoping it would be either. Although I was in my forties, I had never completed a formal budget before. Not sure why I had avoided it for so long. Forecasting and budgeting for the next seven years with our mediation counselor actually took away a lot of the stress I was holding on to by not knowing the real picture.*
>
> —Amy

Making a budget for your new reality doesn't have to be as scary as you think it's going to be. To help you with this, we created a budget worksheet, which you can find in the Resources section in the back of the book, as well as online at www.exwivesguide.com.

Many of you would rather pull out your well-manicured fingernails than create a budget and stare reality in the face. We, the Ex-Wives, would be included in the "many," as we knew the fingernails we would be pulling out would most likely no longer be well-manicured, due to having to afford other stuff, like, for example, food.

Once you complete your new budget, if the numbers aren't pretty, it's better to stare (okay, more like gulp wine and squint out one eye) your new reality in the face. Sure, there might be a little freaking out at first as you try to figure out how you are going to live on that budget, but as the shock quickly settles you will most likely feel an overwhelming renewed sense of purpose. Putting your head in the sand about financial matters is not only a bad idea, it could also lead to financial devastation if you're not careful. Bottom line: develop your budget, get a new game plan, and, it bears repeating, go make that money, honey!

Worksheets and Checklists

Don't reinvent the wheel! We've created checklists and worksheets to help you get organized. You can download them on our website, www.exwivesguide.com, and find them in the Resources section in the back of the book.

- Accounts worksheet
- Copies of documents and paperwork checklist
- Budget worksheet
- Personal expenses spreadsheet
- Personal income spreadsheet

Choose Your Crew

{*a.k.a. your "peeps"*}

Choose wisely or your lifeboat will sink.

"You cannot change the people around you, but you can change the people you choose to be around."

—Anonymous

In the middle of divorcing my husband I broke up with my mom. "Disconnect with love" was the advice given to me by my counselor. My mom resisted. But truth be told, she was driving me insane. I had enough voices going off in my head, not to mention my mother chiming in as the peanut gallery. I could barely keep my thoughts straight. Anytime I talked to her I felt stressed, defensive, and argumentative. I can't blame my mom for being overprotective. I get it. She had been through divorce, so she wanted to help me in every way possible. I knew she meant well and that her words were coming from a place of love, but it didn't matter. I needed a break. My mother was in "mama bear" mode.

—Holiday

We titled this chapter "Choose Your Crew," because as we all saw in the movie *Titanic*, a lifeboat will only hold so many people before it sinks. In addition, you need people in your boat who will help you repair holes, steer you to safety, and will keep on rowing. During divorce your circle of influence is your lifeboat, and the crew is the group of people you choose to allow on board. Be mindful of who you allow on board and be very selective. If you wouldn't depend on these people to pitch in when your boat hits the perfect storm, kick them overboard. They don't belong in your lifeboat.

The challenge with certain people (for example, Holiday's mom) is that they are too close to you. Your pain is their pain. If you are crying or hurt, they want to cry along with you. If you are angry, they are pissed. You can't call this person just to vent; they love you too much to listen without feeling your emotions alongside you. They want to solve every little problem and take away every bit of sadness, anger, and frustration you're facing. Not everything that comes out of your mouth during divorce will need this level of solving, though. In fact, very little will need that Code Red kind of solution or attention. The vast majority of it will just require someone who will listen.

This isn't to say your closest family members shouldn't be a part of your crew, just be aware of how these relationships affect your overall mental health. So take Holiday's counselor's advice: sometimes you need to disconnect with love. It will be the best decision for both of you. Your "breakup" won't last long, but it will be long enough for you to establish boundaries for your relationship.

Friends

Your friends are typically lifelines during a divorce. Below you'll find descriptions of the types of friends you'll want rowing side by side with you in your lifeboat.

Fun Friend—This beloved friend will get you out of those yoga pants you have worn for about two days too long, off the sofa, and out and about into the land of the living. They will be the one to make you a divorce mix that includes all your faves, along with the standards (Madonna's "Respect Yourself" and "You Oughta Know" by Alanis Morissette—you get the idea) and then roll down the windows as the two of you sing loudly while hitting the town for a night out. This friend will bring a smile to your face and remind you of who you really are as a person deep down inside.

Safe House Friend—This is the friend you call when all you want to do is curl up on a sofa, eat massive amounts of anything that has more fat grams than hours in a day, and recount every single detail of every single thing that is wrong to someone you know has your back. This person is your safe house; they will protect you and your feelings. They have no interest in helping you see the bright side if you're upset. They know their job as a friend is to only focus on how you're feeling at that moment. Your secrets are always safe with them. Bonus, this type of friend would rather stay in on a Friday night anyway, so your last-minute call is music to their ears.

Straight Shooter—If you ask this friend, "Does my butt look big in this skirt?" they will actually answer, "Yes. Huge." We all need a straight-shooter friend while going through a divorce. This friend will not only let you know when you're heading for a ride on the Crazy Train, but will slap the ticket out of your hand and drag you out of the station.

It's best not to call this friend on the days you feel super emotional. They will tell you to stop looking at your wedding photos and get out of your wedding dress stat; you are being pathetic. No matter how you act they will label it accurately, and having a trusted friend take control of the reins and steer you toward reality is priceless during this time in your life.

Listener Friend—We all have that one friend that is a super-duper-good listener. You know the one. You can rant for hours on the phone about how crappy your soon-to-be ex is for not noticing your new highlights because he's just jealous you're actually taking care of yourself now, or something deeper, like you're seriously considering running away and never ever coming back, and they don't hang up. They will listen to everything your little mouth can spew out, help sort it out until it makes sense, and then recite a motivational quote.

They won't tell you what you need to do next, and, more importantly, they won't tell you how you should feel. Because they know it's not your story that matters, they are listening to you (as in deep down, past all this shrieking and admitting and sobbing, to the real you), and that's what matters. This friend is invaluable.

In the Weeds Friend—This is the friend that will help you bury the body. Just kidding! Well, they will at least help you bury the voodoo doll they helped you hand stitch and then torture with pins. This friend wants to help you move forward, and they will jump in and stay at your house for a couple of days to make sure you do so. They are not afraid of your day-to-day problems; their goal is to help you clear back the weeds so you can marvel again at the big picture.

They understand that to get from A to Z you have to go through all the other letters of the alphabet first. Need to go to your counseling appointment but not sure who's going to watch the kids that night? No problem, this friend makes it all happen. They hold your hand throughout the entire process, whether it's clenching or swinging, because they know they can help you the most by doing some of the heavy lifting.

In my opinion, family sees you for who you used to be and who you are today. Friends tend to see you for who you should or will be. It's as if they have had a secret viewing into the depths of your soal and the universe has sent them the key to help you unlock that authentic girl out from where she's hiding.

—Valerie

We know that there are many types of friends out there, and any friend that adds value at this point in your life should be considered a blessing. No matter what type of friends or family you choose to have by your side, you should also follow these suggested guidelines.

Be Selective

Friends, family, and random acquaintances will come crawling out of the woodwork when they find out you're getting divorced. Beware, girlfriend. This is not the time to spill the beans to people you don't trust. Remember, whatever you say or do can and will possibly be held against you.

That "Debbie Downer" friend you've known for more than twenty years and stay friends with for longevity's sake? Avoid her. The aunt that keeps calling you because she was divorced thirty years ago and still talks nonstop about how her ex ruined her life and caused her to gain 100 pounds? Email her that you're just not up to talking on the phone these days or checking email, thank her for her sweet thoughts, and tell her you will be out of contact for a while. The friend you and your soon-to-be ex both know at the club who is more of a frenemy than a friend? Every time she approaches you pretend you're having a coughing fit and run to the ladies' lounge.

You're trying to keep your lifeboat afloat. Anyone who normally pokes holes, even when you're not depending on an oversized rubber tube to get you to safety while sharks are lurking below, is o-u-t, out! If they can't understand that this is time you need for yourself, then they're probably not people you need in your new life.

Expect to lose friends during this process. The "family friends" you used to vacation with will feel the ripple effect of your divorce. Don't be surprised or hurt if they go MIA. The feelings of loss are real during divorce. Along with the end of your marriage will come the end of some friendships. It's sad, but true. The best advice we can give you is to keep the people you trust the most close to you.

Boundaries

The ability to set (and enforce) boundaries will make or break you. This is serious stuff. Not to be taken lightly, this word packs a mean punch.

Boundaries are the rules and guidelines you establish for yourself—a general outline of the behavior you will, and will not, accept. This also includes your response to any behavior that may violate your limits.

Boundaries need to be established in all aspects of your life, especially when it comes to the people you surround yourself with. When it comes to choosing your crew, the boundaries you set are vital to your survival. It's amazing how family, friends, and even random acquaintances suddenly have advice and will try to influence someone (you!) going through divorce.

Keep in mind that sometimes the people who love you the most are the ones you need to distance yourself from.

If a family member or friend is closely involved in your situation, it will be hard for them to maintain rational thinking, especially when they see you upset. Continue to focus on surrounding yourself with people who lift you up. Your lifeboat is on rocky water, and you need a stable crew.

Teamwork Makes the Dream Work

Family and friends you trust will emotionally help you during this time, but you also need a team of professionals. Your needs may be different depending on your personal circumstances, but at the very least we recommend having the following professionals on your divorce "team":

- Family law attorney (nonnegotiable!)
- Divorce financial planner
- Counselor or therapist

Divorce Attorney (The Captain)

An experienced divorce attorney can make or break your divorce process. This is the most important member of your team. We have written an entire chapter on how to choose an attorney, but, ultimately, you should hire a qualified divorce lawyer with extensive experience in cases like yours (for example, custody, high net worth, etc.).

Divorce Financial Planner (It's all about the "Benjamins")

Unfortunately, what you've heard is probably true. Far too many women end up broker than broke after their divorce. More often than not, the woman is the one who gets the short end of the stick when it comes to the money, the new debt, the lifestyle, you name it. Lucky for you, we've already made some really stupid mistakes, and we've written this book to make sure you don't do the same thing. You're welcome.

A divorce financial planner is a professional trained in the details and legalities of divorce. This is their specialty. Already have a family financial planner? Tread carefully. If your financial planner worked for you during your marriage, he/she may or may not be as loyal or as focused on you and your best interests at this time. It's best to find a third party, one who has not had prior interactions with your soon-to-be ex.

We can't emphasize this enough: do not hire a regular financial planner, fancy accountant, or CPA right now. You need someone who specializes in divorce. They will know the common pitfalls, recommend structuring of debts, assets, and settlement payout options, such as a QDRO (qualified domestic relations order) or sliding scale alimony, to name a few. Think of them as the soldier on the battlefield who knows there will be bloodshed and loss, but has an aerial view of the past, present, and future, and is going to chart the best possible map of how you can get to your future with the minimum amount of casualties.

It's their job to make sure you're financially prepared now, as well as in the future. Divorce financial planners work closely with your attorney, analyzing the short- and long-term financials of your settlement, as well as varying tax obligations, etc. They will work to protect your assets and provide financial planning strategies for your life post-divorce.

If you and your soon-to-be ex don't have that many assets or savings to protect, a good neutral friend who is financially savvy is a viable alternative. They should create spreadsheets that figure premarital, marital, and post-marital financial obligations, debts, and assets. Then they can paint the picture of where you and your soon-to-be ex need to be headed, and how best to get there. Be advised, they most likely won't know specific divorce implications, but they can at least break down the figures on spreadsheets and forecast expenses and financial needs. You can then work with your attorney more effectively to create a settlement that won't leave you financially ruined.

Counselor/Therapist (But . . . I'm not the crazy one!)

Does the word "counseling" give you the heebie-jeebies? Yeah, us too, until we tried it.

I always had a negative connotation with "counseling" as a kid and young adult. It wasn't until I had my first baby when I realized, "Hmm, my friends don't really want to hear this crap, and if I told my parents what I really wanted to say they'd probably send a police officer to come and look for me."

I finally broke down to my neighbor one day (bless her heart). She stuck her counselor's business card in my mailbox the next day. The rest is history. I've always told my counselor she would be the one person I'd bring with me to a deserted island (other than my children, well, at least one of them, just kidding . . . kinda). My girlfriend (said neighbor) and I still joke about how we would love to invite her for a sleepover and just pick her brain all night, then we could analyze our dreams in the morning over coffee and pancakes. Ah, I digress.

In all seriousness, my counselor has been a source of guidance for me several times in my life, not just divorce. In fact, I had been seeing her long before divorce was on the horizon. Now, that doesn't mean she was completely shocked when I busted through her door on a rainy Wednesday afternoon, announcing, "It's over!" Shock was hardly her response. In fact, it appeared to be more like a sign of relief—remember, this poor woman had listened to me for several years.

—Holiday

After my second divorce I knew I needed to talk to someone professional about why I was going to be officially divorced twice and was just shy of thirty. There seemed to be a common denominator there, and it seemed to be me. After working with Helen, it was as if someone finally turned on the "Oh, that makes sense now" switch. Sure we talked about what happened in my past (let's save those daddy issues for another book), and what happened with both the failed marriages I left (hello, needing to be wanted), but we also talked about what I could do to try and make better decisions.

Just having someone I could let it all spill out to once a week, who wouldn't judge me, for those two years, was priceless. Even when I ran back to her comfy, now reupholstered chair five years later because I was facing my third divorce, she helped guide me through understanding a time in my life I didn't think I'd ever fully wrap my head around.

—Valerie

A counselor or therapist will be your source of safety. You are safe to share your authentic feelings, fears, sadness, emotional challenges, just about anything and everything that's on your mind. A professional counselor will help you navigate these experiences and provide you with coping mechanisms and strategies.

When choosing a counselor or therapist, the most important thing is for you to feel comfortable. Counseling is typically a very intimate experience. If you don't feel comfortable with the other person, you're wasting your time.

It's like going on a really, really bad date, and at the end you get stuck with the bill. Now what fun is that?

Make sure your counselor or therapist is someone you feel you can trust and not hide anything from. If you don't share the full story, again you're wasting your time, and chances are you're not fooling them anyway. You need someone who will not only listen to you, but who will also speak to you in a manner that will motivate you personally to move toward a better life.

> *The first counselor I met with seemed to be soft-spoken and gentle. After two sessions it was clear that all he was doing was making me want to cry and eat Chick-fil-A as soon as I left his office. Although he was qualified and kind, it just wasn't my style. I then reached out to my insurance and they recommended a couple of counselors that were close by. I called all three and within fifteen minutes one had called me back to discuss what I was looking for. Within two minutes I knew she spoke the language I needed to hear—the language that would help get me through my divorce. If I wasn't going to settle for a husband that was a bad fit, why would I settle for a counselor that wasn't a good fit?*
>
> —Joy

When it comes to mental health, there are a variety of professional options to choose from. We will translate for you.

- Psychiatrist: A medical doctor specializing in preventing, diagnosing, and treating mental illness. Licensed to write prescriptions. Monitors the effects of mental illness on the physical conditions of the patient (blood pressure, etc.). May refer patient to counseling for therapy in addition to medication.
- Psychologist: Has a doctoral degree in psychology (the study of the mind and behaviors), however, is not a medical doctor. Qualified to perform counseling, psychotherapy, psychological testing, and provide treatment for mental disorders. Unable to write prescriptions (in most states). Will most likely provide psychotherapy for patient and collaborate with psychiatrist for medical treatment.
- Licensed Mental Health Counselor: A mental health professional with a master's degree in psychology, counseling, or related field, licensed by the state. Qualified to evaluate and treat mental problems via counseling or psychotherapy.
- Clinical Social Worker: A professional with a master's degree in social work, as well as training on diagnosing and evaluating mental illness. Can provide psychotherapy as well as case management for patients. May also serve as an advocate for patients and their families.

**Original source: www.webmd.com*

Don't let these titles scare you. There are several different avenues in the mental health field, so choosing the professional that will best serve your personal needs is important. Talk to your physician about your circumstances and ask for referrals. If you have health insurance, contact your provider and ask about mental health coverage.

> *A friend suggested I call my insurance provider to see if meeting with a therapist was included in my health plan. I had no idea that was part of my coverage. Bonus: not only was it covered, but I was quickly approved for unlimited sessions that calendar year and only a small co-pay. Who knew? Either I was really messed up, or I just had really great insurance. Either way, win-win!*
>
> —Valerie

As a part of your divorce team, your counselor will help you manage this crazy emotional tidal wave otherwise known as divorce. Don't underestimate the power of a positive mental state of mind. You're going to need some serious emotional support, even if you think you've got it all together right now. Since a counselor or therapist offers an outside view, they're better able to provide you with unbiased opinions and perspectives. If you have children, we will go into more detail on counseling for kids in Chapter 8, "Kids' Club."

Once you have a list of referrals, visit a few offices and choose the person you feel most comfortable with. Give it a chance. You've got nothing to lose and everything to gain.

Divorce isn't easy, but having a solid divorce team helps make things manageable. Hire the best professionals you can afford to protect you and fight for you. It will be money extremely well spent.

Oh Captain, My Captain

{*hiring an attorney*}

Cowritten by "Captain" Carol S. Baskin, Esq.

"The jury consists of twelve persons chosen to decide who has the better lawyer."

—Robert Frost

Navigating a divorce without an attorney is like setting sail on a sinking ship; it's not a good plan. Girlfriend, you absolutely need to have an attorney, especially if you have children and/or assets to protect.

Not only do we share an ex-husband, but we also shared a divorce attorney. It seemed only fitting to weigh in with our expert counsel for advice on hiring an attorney and what to expect from a legal perspective during the divorce process. Carol was our "Captain" because she made sure the ship never sank. She still does. We trust her—you should, too!

Top Three Reasons You Need an Attorney:

From the captain herself, Carol Baskin, Esq.

1. When going through a divorce you will be dealing with a lot of emotions that will color your perspective and may lead you to make some bad decisions. An attorney is there to represent your interests and to help you through the emotional land mines. We are here to help

you understand the logic in your choices and to guide you down the correct path.

2. Unless you have a law degree, you will not understand the rules of engagement. You may enter into agreements that may not be enforceable by the court, or worse yet, once agreed to can't be undone after there is a court order.
3. The attorney you hire should have experience in the court system you are getting divorced in. They can advise you as to what to expect from the judge, or judges, you are assigned to. Judges are human beings with their own value systems and perspectives, which will play a large role in how they are likely to interpret and decide on a case before them. It is imperative that the facts, as well as the situation, are presented in a professional manner and in a light that the court will find both reasonable and acceptable so that you can prevail in your settlement or litigation.

Captain Carol explains, "It is unethical and unacceptable for an attorney to represent both the husband and wife in a divorce. Get your own attorney and discuss your entire financial situation. It is common for spouses to make threats; the kind of threats your husband is probably making right now if you are in the process of a divorce. The judge is the one who will make a decision about what will happen, not your husband. All of the assets and income in the marriage must be considered. The value of a business begun and run during marriage is an asset that is divided by the court. Talk to an attorney before you jump to any conclusions about who will have to pay what."

Mistakes the Ex-Wives Have Made:

- **LegalZoom:** Don't laugh, some people really try.
- **Uncontested Divorce:** This is only an option if you don't have any assets or children or represent that .001 percent of humanity.
- **Sharing an attorney:** In Fantasy Land you and your husband initially dream up this fabulous idea of marching into an attorney's office and proceeding with the divorce together to save money. It sounds like a great idea, but in the real world you need your own captain, girlfriend.

Things You Should Look for When Hiring an Attorney:

Experience/Expertise: Family and Divorce Law

Would you hire your hairdresser to change the oil in your car? No. Same thing goes for attorneys. Any divorce attorney you consider should have substantial experience with (or knowledge of) divorce and/or family law. The Google search key words are "family law attorney in [your home town, or state]."

Ability to Communicate

What's worse than a friend who always sends your calls to voice mail? An attorney who ignores you. Trust us, you want to be sure your attorney will effectively communicate with you. It's important for them to be accessible and prompt in responding to your requests and/or inquiries. It's important that your personalities mesh well. Keep in mind, sometimes opposites attract. For example, if you're timid and shy, you may work better with a more aggressive attorney.

Assessment of Fees

When you make your initial appointment with the divorce attorney, you should inquire about a consultation fee. Some attorneys do brief initial consultations for free; however, most experienced divorce attorneys will charge between one hundred and four hundred dollars as a consultation fee, or will charge their normal hourly rate. Find out what the attorney's hourly rate is, what the up-front retainer will be, whether any portion of the retainer is refundable if it is not used, and how often you can expect to receive invoices that detail their hourly charges and expenses. At the very least, comparison shop so you know the going rates in your area. You don't have to just take the cheapest, and paying the most does not necessarily mean you'll be getting the most, but you should spend time interviewing a variety of attorneys, and getting familiar with the costs involved. Do not be afraid to ask for payment arrangements based on your financial situation—fees can be negotiable.

Intuition

Okay, this may sound odd, given the fact that you may now be feeling as though you didn't make the right choice in a spouse, but follow your gut.

Plain and simple. If you don't get a good feeling from a particular lawyer and/or firm, then continue your search. Just like choosing a wedding dress: you might end up with the first one you tried on, but you've got to try on several to make sure the first one was "The One." You need to be 100 percent confident with your legal representation, so be sure to follow your intuition along with listening to your gut. If something doesn't seem right, then it probably isn't. And always remember, your attorney works for you, not the other way around. There are certain ethical standards to which family law practitioners must adhere. Hiring a lawyer is like being on a job interview. Don't fall prey to condescension. You have done nothing wrong, and your attorney should respect you and do their job and represent your interests to the best of their ability.

When Is It Time to Hire an Attorney? (Hint: The time is NOW)

Captain Carol advises: "Unfortunately, most individuals put this off too long. Frankly, the sooner you start getting some advice from an experienced attorney to set proper expectations in the event of a separation or divorce, the better you will be able to handle the situation when and if it actually occurs.

"By doing this you are not admitting defeat to the relationship. Sometimes actually speaking to a knowledgeable attorney might assist you in finding out how to preserve and save your marriage.

"As attorneys, we all should know the law, but we vary greatly in our approach and dealings with our clients. You have to determine who is your right match, and doing this before (and if) you decide to go through the process of divorce will definitely help you."

We say: Amen! Hallelujah! Word. Wish we had spoken to an attorney before the you-know-what had already hit and was swirling around in the fan!

I Know Someone Who Knows Someone . . .

Captain Carol says to be mindful that:

"Your friends and family will have an ample amount of advice, but unfortunately most of it will be ineffective for a number of reasons:

- They may relay horror stories that may inhibit your personal decisions.
- They may lead you to have unrealistic expectations in regard to your specific situation.

I'm not suggesting you underestimate the value of friends or family, just be cautious; their situations most likely vary drastically from yours. They may, however, be an excellent resource in helping you to find the right match for an attorney that fits your needs and personality."

Take it from us, once you start the process of divorce and tell family, friends, etc., you'll quickly realize that everyone (your hairdresser, mechanic, and the person behind you in line at the grocery store) will want to contribute their two cents. Don't get caught in the middle. Find the right attorney for you and only take advice from people you would trade places with.

Get the Scoop

Now is the time to ask your friends or family who have experienced divorce for recommendations. Most people are quick and open to discussing their personal experiences with their previous or present attorney and the law firm they represent.

Here is a list of the most important things Captain Carol believes you should find out about these referrals:

- The personality of the professional counsel they are recommending
- The experience level of the attorney that represented them
- How comfortable they were in communicating with their attorney and the firm staff

Unfortunately, we both forgot to ask several of these key questions when getting referrals. We mostly asked, "Are they a badass, and do they take AmEx?" Because of this, we have created a handy-dandy form (found in the back of the book and at www.exwivesguide.com) you can use so you won't forget. You'll thank us big time for this.

You've got recommendations from people you trust and you've done your homework. Check and check. Being the C.E.O. we know you are (**C**hief **E**mpress **O**rganizer), you've picked up the phone and contacted several firms. You have spoken with the staff at the firm and possibly with one of the attorneys directly. The search is almost over. Now, pick up the phone and schedule an appointment or two for consultations.

Now is NOT the Time for Bargain Shopping

Captain Carol warns: "Don't select an attorney just because he, or she, offers free consultations. They may be great and knowledgeable attorneys, or they may be just starting out in their career and need to hone their skills.

"If you and your husband have any assets to speak of, or if custody is involved, you will absolutely need an attorney who knows domestic relations law backwards and forwards. Don't sell your whole future to the lowest bidder; place it with the best bidder and fit for you." Just like most things in life, you get what you pay for.

When Holiday was looking for an attorney, her mother's exact words were, "This is NOT the time to go bargain shopping." She was right. This doesn't necessarily mean the most expensive attorney is the right one. (Valerie can attest to that!) However, you are setting yourself (and your children) up for the future. As in, for the rest of your lives—don't F this up.

Hire the best attorney you can afford. Save the bargain shopping for the Bullseye's Playground at Target.

Be Prepared (Yep, we're beating this like a dead horse)

Before you have your initial consultation with an attorney, Captain Carol notes that you'll most likely be asked to fill out some preliminary paperwork. Her advice: "Do not take this assignment lightly. Work hard to be as complete as possible. You will be rewarded with the attorney being able to assess your situation much more thoroughly and give you a clearer insight as to what the future might hold for you. We do not have crystal balls; we work with information. The more we have, the better we can assess and discuss the most probable outcome for you, the client.

"You may not wish to think of your marriage as a business partnership, but in effect, it will be seen that way in the court system. If you have tax returns, checking account records, investment records, copies of debts and values for property (for real estate, investments, and personal property) at your disposal, make copies to provide to the attorney on your first visit. This is a treasure trove for us in assisting you to understand what may, or may not, happen as a result of an eventual divorce."

Refer back to Chapter 5, "Get Organized, Girl," for a complete list of all documents you will need to gather up. We've even given you organizational tips. If you followed our advice and organized all the paperwork, you can hand over the folder, binder, or "treasure trove" as Captain Carol calls it, to your prospective counsel. Our guess is that they will try and hire you as their client, not the other way around! We'll say it again: this will save you thousands of dollars and hundreds of headaches. Smart women save their money and energy for the things that deserve it.

What about custody?

If you think your husband is going to fight you in the area of custody, which is normally one of the biggest concerns among parents, according to Captain Carol, you will need to convey to your prospective attorney the following important points:

1. What is your typical parenting style for the child (or children) and what is your husband's parenting style?
2. Does one parent currently spend a considerably larger amount of time with the child (children) than the other?
3. How do you divide up the responsibilities?
4. Is a child particularly bonded to one parent more than the other parent?
5. Is one parent the fun parent and the other the disciplinarian?
6. Do your children have any special needs and, if so, which parent spends their time addressing those needs?
7. Are any of your children old enough to make a legal declaration as to which parent they wish to live with?
8. Are you prepared to accept the situation if they do not wish to live with you?

Captain Carol states, "Be sure to have these answers ready to give to the attorney at your initial consultation. They will use these as insight as to how they may help you now, as well as in the future."

This is where we, as ex-wives with children, need to warn you: don't be surprised if your spouse uses custody to threaten you. This is a scare tactic and it's a "go-to" manipulation strategy men use to flex their muscles. Remember, he's going to do anything he can to push your buttons. If you're like most mothers in this world, your children are the hottest button of all. If we had a dollar for every girlfriend who has called us in hysterics regarding her husband's custody threats we would be dirty, filthy rich. During this time of crisis, it is more important than ever to be the best parent you can be. Keep your composure and try your best to be level-headed. Leave the custody threats to your attorney—yet another reason to make sure you find the right fit for you!

> *Every time my ex and I would fight during our separation he would threaten me that he was going to get full custody of our children. I would cry myself to sleep almost every night. As soon as I hired an attorney, I told him what was happening. He suggested I record it once, save it, and then pay no attention to it. He also said I should tell him that threat is not going to work anymore. It worked like a charm.*
>
> —Denise

Consultation Day

You've got your ducks in a row and your files are prepared. The day of your consultation has arrived, but suddenly you have cold feet.

Why?

No one on this earth wants to believe they have made a mistake, and you are no different. You have not made a mistake. No action or choice is ever wasted—it brings us closer to who we are supposed to be through life lessons. Each of us evolves in our own unique way as we age. You could no more predict how you or your spouse would evolve than you could predict the winning numbers for Wednesday's Powerball lottery. Sometimes our aging brings us closer, other times it pulls us apart as our interests and life goals change. Maturity and clarity also set in. Sadly, this sometimes only happens for one spouse and not the other. Don't blame yourself.

You made this appointment for a reason. It is one hour of your life. Now go to the appointment and find out what the professional has to say.

Captain Carol's Tip: "Bring a notebook and pen to take notes or a recording device (with attorney's permission) during your first meeting. Be diligent about taking notes and writing down the attorney's response as you go through your list of questions.

"Speaking of questions . . . don't be afraid to ask! You will not be able to address how to deal with your issues properly if you do not have the requisite information. Is the professional giving you their undivided attention, or are they trying to impress you with how busy they are or how many people work for them? Be impressed with eye contact, not a two-page firm roster."

Captain Carol's Heartfelt Advice: "You should be the only thing that matters to him, or her, when you are with that person. This is your time and it should be honored. If not, look elsewhere."

The Ex-Wives' Tip:

If you're too nervous to go by yourself, ask a friend or someone you trust to join you . . . especially if you're experiencing nausea and/or diarrhea (yes, this is very normal). Two memories and notetakers are better than one. Make sure the person you bring can keep you on task and make the most of your time, especially if you have to excuse yourself to go to the restroom every ten minutes.

Expect to be nervous and anxious the first time you meet with your attorney. Arrive early and settle in prior to your scheduled appointment time. Be prepared with your list of questions and the areas of concern you want to discuss. This is an excellent way to determine if they are interested in hearing what you have to say, or if the attorney is only interested in hearing their own voice and their rehearsed sound bites. Shy away from the latter!

Valerie recalls an initial consultation with a potential attorney: "It seemed the counsel was mostly concerned with showing me the one-of-a-kind view from their spectacular office overlooking downtown Atlanta, rather than discussing the major issues I was having pertaining to my already-filed divorce. That should have been my red flag: racking up billable hours to pay for that beautiful view was more important to them than helping build a better view of life for me in the future."

Questions to ask before writing a big, fat check:

1. Ask about the attorney's experience in the handling of domestic relations cases.
   - Is it the primary focus of the firm, or do they practice other areas of law as well?
   - Do they practice in the court system where your case will be filed and heard (highly recommended)?
2. Who will you be working with?
   - Paralegals, secretaries, associate counsel, interns, etc.?
   - What hourly rate will you be charged for each professional? (Rates differ. The more experience and degrees, the higher the bill rate.)
3. How will you communicate with the office and with the attorney?
   - What is the best method of communication for after office hours or on the weekend?
   - Will they schedule telephone appointments?
   - What are the charges for email communications?
4. Ask important questions about your retainer.
   - Is your retainer refundable?
   - When will you be expected to replenish your retainer?
5. How long is the process likely to take from the beginning to the end of the litigation?
6. Will your action require expert testimony? (This may be the case in hotly contested custody actions or in actions involving complex assets and/or closely held corporations.)
   - What is likely to be the cost for these experts?
   - How will that be funded?
   - Are you or your attorney responsible for hiring the professional?
   - What is the benefit to you as to which method is done?

Money Matters

Don't be afraid to ask about fees and the general costs associated with litigation. Remember, you are the one entering into a contract with this firm. You are ultimately liable for the associated fees. Though the firm may seek fees from your spouse, nothing is guaranteed in that endeavor. Try to have a realistic understanding of those expenses prior to engaging the firm so that you will be able to make the best business decision for yourself.

Captain Carol says: "You will be expected to pay a 'retainer' prior to the firm starting work on your behalf. This can be modest, or a very substantial sum of money based on the work the attorney and firm believe they will have to conduct on your case. Read the contract that is given to you to sign! Take it home with you to review when you are less stressed. No firm should be pressuring you to sign on the dotted line without you having a full understanding of the office procedures and practices. Do not feel compelled to make a decision that day. The simple truth is that the day you do make a decision is the right day, and not a moment before."

Captain Carol's Tip for avoiding an oil spill: If the retainer is a substantial sum, ask if it will be escrowed, entitling you to a refund in the event the entire sum is not used.

Communication Is Key

Before you walk out of the attorney's office, Captain Carol strongly encourages you to "find out how accessible the attorney will be in case you need to contact them during the litigation process. Most of us now use email for almost all instantaneous communications with our clients. If we are both clear as attorney and client at what works best for both of our schedules, then we are more likely to be more efficient."

Captain Carol's office policy you will dig: "Our staff designates a specific time for a client to call into the office to speak with us about their case. The benefit of this is that the file is given to us prior to the designated time, and we are able to review and check for any and all updates so we can provide you with the most up-to-date information."

Knowing up front how Carol's office operated required me to condense my questions and really use my time with her wisely. Before reaching out (via email or phone) I made sure I knew EXACTLY what I was asking. It was intimidating at first, but over time I realized this was a helpful exercise for me because I was always prepared. This also helped to keep my bill down!

—Holiday

Listen to Your Gut

Captain Carol says to answer these questions immediately following your appointment. (If you vomited or had diarrhea during your consultation, take a Pepto pronto, then answer these questions.)

1. How did you feel when you left the office?
2. Were you heard, or were you preached to?
3. Did the attorney explain the law to you, or patronize you?
4. Were you criticized for your conduct, or accepted as you are with all your flaws? (Trust us, we all have them.)
5. Did you feel rushed, or were you allowed to communicate fully with the attorney?
6. Did you become comfortable with the attorney you were speaking with and feel that you would be able to tell that professional everything (and she does mean everything) that may have to be revealed about your life?

Again, refer to the handy-dandy form at www.exwivesguide.com that we created for you to jot down all the stuff you may be likely to forget. We know this because we FORGOT! You will be so stressed and emotionally charged; writing it down will help lasso those runaway thoughts back into the corral forming in your head, cowgirl. Yeehaw!

One Size Does Not Fit All

Captain Carol's favorite advice to our girlfriends: "You are unique. You are special and do not fit into a box so that an outcome can be predicted prior to a final decree. Yes, as attorneys we do look at generalities and the initial parameters of your case to determine major issues we predict to encounter on your behalf. If we skip that step, we cannot properly prepare to make the necessary decisions, which will ultimately affect your future post-divorce. Remember, knowledge and communication with 100 percent transparency is the key to the outcome you are seeking. I wish you good luck."

Don't forget to use the Questions to Ask Your Lawyer form, which you can find in the back of the book and online at www.exwivesguide.com.

Kids' Club

{*how to help the kiddos*}

Cowritten by Sheri M. Siegel, PhD, licensed clinical psychologist

"Divorce isn't such a tragedy. A tragedy's staying in an unhappy marriage, teaching your children the wrong things about love."

—Jennifer Weiner

Welcome to the Kids' Club. The one club you probably never wanted your child to have to join and your child never wanted to be a part of. Divorcing parents already feel guilty for just about everything; now throw in the kids and it's a downright sobfest.

But as all of us know, we must remain strong for the sake of our little or not-so-little ones. To help us with this chapter we turned to Sheri M. Siegel, PhD, a licensed clinical psychologist who specializes in family counseling, for her professional advice. She has been practicing privately for more than twenty-five years in Metro Atlanta. She often testifies as an expert witness in court, so she knows her stuff, to say the least.

The Most Important Message for Kids

Dr. Sheri suggests you make it your mission to ensure your children know these three very important things:

1. This is a life change we will work through together.
2. Our love for you as parents is strong and will never change, even though the family is changing.
3. Your best interest is our primary goal.

Below are Dr. Sheri's top pieces of advice. Consider this your ultra-do-and-don't list when it comes to the kids.

Top advice for a mother facing divorce:

Dr. Sheri suggests: "For a mother facing divorce, planning ahead is key. Get answers to as many anticipated questions as possible in place long before talking with the kids. Children remember the moment of being told/finding out forever. That moment needs to be handled very carefully and thoughtfully."

Top advice to a mother in the thick of it:

"To a mother in the midst of divorce, it's imperative to maintain perspective and balance. While the well-being of your children is a primary focus, you must take care of yourself also."

We totally get that. If the children see mommy falling apart, they will feel responsible for taking care of you. You can't take care of others until you take care of you.

Top advice to a mother after the dust settles:

"Throughout the divorce process, and especially afterwards, the relationship you maintain with your ex is crucial to the well-being of your children. Do everything you can to maintain a positive working relationship with him for the sake of the kids. Treat the relationship like a business partnership, and try to disconnect from the emotions you may have towards him. Co-parenting the children is the primary business in the custodial relationship. Regardless of how he acts, remember, you can only control yourself. Your kids are paying attention to how you act, react, and handle yourself in all situations."

Talking with Kids

Dr. Sheri says, "Verbal affirmation is crucial for childhood development. They need to have confidence in what you are telling them. Here are some things your kids need to hear:

- It's not your fault.
- We both love you, and we always will.
- We will work together to minimize the changes in your life—we know you didn't ask for divorce.
- There is nothing you can do to change our decision; it is a grown-up decision and not one you get a vote in. However, there will be plenty of opportunities when you can make decisions."

Top Five Don'ts for a Parent:

1. Don't hate your ex more than you love your children.
2. Don't remain emotionally married after you are legally divorced.
3. Don't tell your children adult details about the marital breakup, especially regarding misconduct or infidelity. Children never need to know this.
4. Don't have too many life changes occur at once if at all possible (moving, changing schools, remarriages, etc.)
5. Don't communicate with your ex through your children, directly or indirectly.

Breaking the News

It's the moment you've been dreading since you made the final decision. That moment your kids will remember forever . . . the moment that will rock their world, and it will never, ever, ever be the same. That moment when once it's been said, there's no turning back.

Telling your kids that you are getting divorced is one of the hardest conversations you will have in your life, if not the hardest. And it's one you shouldn't take lightly.

I still remember vividly, over thirty years later, when my mother sat my brothers and I down to tell us that she and my father were getting divorced. I remember her shaking, looking frail, fighting back tears. I had never seen her that upset before. It made me want to jump out of my chair and run. When I asked her what divorce meant she started crying uncontrollably. I didn't know what divorce was at that point in my life, but I knew it couldn't be something good.

—Jessica

Dr. Sheri says, "Being prepared is crucial to the success of this conversation. A clear and concise strategy should be in place, and it should involve your ex. In a perfect world, both parents can sit down with a plan, already have specific answers to the questions you know the kids will ask, and agree to mutually support each other."

Meeting with a mental health professional who specializes in divorcing and divorced families is ideal to prepare for this. The purpose of pre-divorce meetings is to focus on the best interests of the children. A counselor or therapist can help both parents prepare for the conversation."

We both agree. We both divorced when our children were younger. Valerie's son was three, and Holiday's daughters were two and four. Just because they were younger didn't mean that we wouldn't have to have the "Big Talk" at some point. Thanks to the therapists we were each seeing, we were prepared to keep it together and build our children's confidence.

Because my son was only three when my ex and I divorced, it was as if he didn't know any different. There was mommy's house and daddy's condo. Mommy's car and daddy's car, and so on. One day he was telling me that daddy's condo had a balcony, and I said "I know—you can see the street!" He replied, "How do you know daddy's condo, Mommy?" It was as if he had a mommy and daddy, but we were completely separate entities. Somehow I had dodged having to have the big talk.

It wasn't until he was five that he asked me what a divorce was and if I was I ever married. I explained to him what a divorce was in a definition sort of way, gave him examples of people that we knew who were divorced, and told him that I had been married to his daddy. He had the strangest look on his face, a half smirk of sorts. He then asked "So you loved my daddy like I do?" I replied, "Yes, yes I did."

The ironic part was that his father had just sent me a really mean-spirited email earlier in the day and I wanted to wring his neck, but it was in that very moment I realized, no matter how challenging his father could be, he had given me the thing I love most in the world, my son. And luckily for me my son obviously felt nothing but that love despite our very contentious divorce. It might single-handedly be one of my proudest moments ever.

—Valerie

Dr. Sheri's Tips:

- Strategize and plan the conversation with your ex and be prepared to have the conversation with the children together.
- Sit down with all the children together and maintain a unified front. Even though your marriage is over, you will continue to be a team as co-parents.
- Have predetermined and mutually agreed-upon answers to questions children are likely to ask, such as, "Where will we live?" and "What about Christmas?" Rehearse what you will say, who will be saying it, and ensure both of you are on the same page.
- Keep the conversation short. The kids will be emotional and will tune out quickly.

Dr. Sheri's Thoughts on Family Counseling:

"In a perfect world, as the divorce process starts, the parents enter into custodial counseling electively long before a court order is issued by a judge. It's this divorce counseling that helps the parents stay focused on the children, and working together on the children's behalf instead of focusing on the emotionally heated issues that led to the divorce."

***WARNING:* Do not make arrangements for child counseling without the consent of your ex.**

"I can't tell you how many calls I get from moms (most well-meaning; some trying to sneak behind their ex) to set up counseling for their children," explains Dr. Sheri. "Most divorce arrangements these days involve joint legal custody. Regardless of who has primary custody or final say in medical decisions, if there is joint legal custody, both parents need to sign the consent forms for the children to enter counseling. This is a lawsuit waiting to happen for the mental professional who enters into a case otherwise, unless it is court-ordered by a judge or guardian ad litem."

She says, "Ideally, if children are coming to counseling, it's best for parents to alternate bringing the children so they can feel that both parents care. It also allows both parents to be involved in the counseling process."

Note: Not all children of divorce need counseling. In general, the more unhealthily and heatedly the divorce process is being handled by the parents, the more potential damage could be caused to the children.

Dr. Sheri notes, "It is usually detrimental for children to be in family counseling with both parents in the room at the same time. Usually this is quite stressful for the kids. It can be helpful for the kids to be in the counseling room with both parents in the waiting room area ONLY IF the parents are behaving and not in conflict. Otherwise, it creates a great deal of stress for the children."

Do not quiz the children about their counseling sessions. We think this should be a given, but we know how hard it is to not fully know what our beloved children are thinking and feeling.

"It is horrible to use the kids as spies during sessions," states Dr. Sheri, who shares the following example: "Recently, I was facilitating a reunification session with a daughter and father. The mother hates her ex so much that by default she is teaching her daughter to do so as well. The mother had the daughter secretly record the session so she (the mother) could challenge me regarding the process in the sessions."

Using your children for anything regarding your ex is off limits. Period. If you have one goal or rule for yourself as a parent, let it be this.

Emotional Management

Staying strong

The big question most women ask when it comes to emotional management is, "How can I be strong for my kids when I'm falling apart inside?" All mothers feel this at some point, if not throughout the entire divorce process.

"Get support for yourself and make sure your kids know you are getting support to reduce their worry about you," Dr. Sheri recommends. "They need to see that it's okay to get help. Support can come in many forms, including but certainly not limited to family, friends, formal therapy, support groups, empowerment services (such as Visions Anew, a local organization), places of worship, self-help books, Internet/social media support. This is a great opportunity to teach your kids about coping with adversity."

Dr. Sheri's Top Tip: It is important to not lean on your kids for adult emotional support.

"Keep boundaries clear so your kids do not feel like your therapist, parent, friend, etc. Often, sensitive kids will develop school avoidance behaviors because they feel the need to stay home to take care of the parents they are worried about," she notes.

Take it from Dr. Sheri as well as us, you definitely don't want to head down that road.

Bedtime tears

So, it's the first couple weeks of daddy being gone and your kids are crying at night begging for their daddy. Awesome.

When we asked Dr. Sheri how she recommends handling this, she offered this advice: "It helps to have family photos, memorabilia, etc. in kids' rooms, especially pictures of the child with the parent they aren't with (pictures of the child with mom at dad's house and vice versa). It can also help to have objects that have some meaning to help the child stay connected with the parent they aren't with, such as dad's nightshirt to wear or use as a pillowcase, mom's nightgown or special piece of jewelry, etc."

Sticky questions (like, *Why doesn't daddy live here anymore?*)

"It is very helpful for the kids to hear from the noncustodial parent frequently (ideally, daily), and in many different forms, including calls, texts, Skype, Facetime, letters, etc.

"It can also be helpful to have books for kids on divorce to help normalize the process, books that focus on the kids having two homes now. 'Mom's house and dad's house'—start this type of language early on to prevent the feeling that kids are living with one parent and visiting the other.

"Overall, parents need to normalize the process from the onset and set the goal of helping the kids to adjust to the situation as it is. Kids do not need to feel they have the power to shorten their time with one parent by trying to be with the other. The parents ideally need to work together to help the kids adjust instead of trying to change the schedule.

"Refer to having planned, prepared answers to these types of questions so the answer can be reported and repeated in a nonemotional fashion."

"Dad has a different home now, but it is also your home, because you now have two homes."

Age makes a difference

The ages of the kids, their developmental stage, and gender may all have an impact. Dr. Sheri says it's important to "stay in tune with your child and where your child stands in their current stage of development. For example, a pre-puberty boy may need more time with his dad. This is normal and nothing against mom."

We know how important this was to us. With our children being so young we were worried about scarring them forever, especially during the formative years. Thanks to advice from the counselors we were working with, we read books that focused on children that were age appropriate with our situations, as well as prepared ourselves for regressions and outbursts from toddlers, which we happily report were minimal.

> *Both my boys handled our divorce differently. My ten-year-old wouldn't stop asking when was it a dad weekend. It's all he talked about, which at the time was really hard for me personally. My twelve-year-old acted like my protector and wanted to be by my side at all times to be the problem solver. I had to constantly keep my finger on how their very individual personalities, as well as different ages, played out to help me understand why they were reacting the way they were.*
>
> —Jenny

Changes in Behavior

Warning signs from Dr. Sheri (a.k.a. the flashing neon signs you shouldn't avoid).

Top five most common changes in behavior:

1. Anxiety and/or separation anxiety
2. Defiance and/or opposition
3. Depression
4. Isolation
5. Self-destructive behaviors, such as drugs, drinking, cutting class, and promiscuity

Dr. Sheri notes, "There are so many red flags to look for, and ways kids can exhibit maladjustment behaviorally and emotionally. Stay tuned in to your kids and look for changes or reports of changes (like from teachers). As a general rule, look for changes from the norm with kids and/or exaggerations of their typical behaviors and emotions.

"Keep an open door for conversations and make sure your kids have key people well positioned in their lives to lean on if they are not going to talk with you directly. That includes teachers, clergy, parents of friends, coaches, etc.," she suggests. "The saying 'It takes a village to raise a child' is true, especially during a divorce."

Sibling Love

Children react differently to divorce. Don't be surprised if siblings are affected differently, as was seen in Jenny's case above.

"Just as each child is different, each of your children will act differently toward the divorce," Dr. Sheri explains. "Some inherently are more resilient than others. Some will adapt better. Some will lean on each other for support. Some will only lean on others outside the family. It shouldn't be a surprise when siblings don't react the same way."

She adds, "Note: in the cases I have seen where siblings get split up, this is usually quite detrimental. Siblings for the most part need to go back and forth between parents as a sibling unit."

Things to Document as a Parent

Although you will be taking copious notes at every turn in your divorce, you will want to keep this level of vigilance away from kids, according to Dr. Sheri.

"Try to not assume that your ex will be a poor parent, abusive parent, or neglectful parent, even if he was a crazy husband," suggests Dr. Sheri.

"As far as actual documentation and level of detail to keep, consult with your legal representative; just keep the note-taking far away from kids' eyes and certainly don't have it be their responsibility to report on the other parent."

One thing to remember is any and all notes should be largely taken to help determine what is best for the child, not for yourself. Anything you document should help the counsel, courts, and therapists get a fair and accurate picture of something that could be detrimental to your child. Detrimental is your child stating dad left them alone all day to go out to the bars. Your child stating dad was on his phone for a while Saturday morning is not.

Custody/Visitation: (Ideal way to determine)

Dr. Sheri says an ideal way to determine custody and visitation would be for the husband and wife to have discussions first. "This is helpful in the presence of an experienced mental health professional to help the divorcing couple stay focused on what will work for the kids," she notes.

We know the ideal way is not always the realistic way. In fact, after listening to all the women we spoke to and interviewed while writing this book, we think it's safe to say about half worked solely with their attorneys and counsel on determining custody and visitation plans. The women with the most success were the most realistic and did what was best for the children based on schooling, activities, and special needs. The women with the least success, and most frustration, were the ones who weren't okay with the fact that change was going to happen. Not just for their kids, but for themselves.

As we have said all along, change is inevitable. So be the bright, shining example we know you are for your kiddos, and continue to put their true needs ahead of yours.

We'll dive into more detail on this in the next chapter, so take Dr. Sheri's advice and try to work this out with your soon-to-be ex, ideally at the onset of your divorce, using professional counselors to help you.

Optimal Way to Explain

Dr. Sheri suggests, "Once decisions are made that impact the kids, discussions with the kids can now take place."

Make sure to include important details such as:

1. When the separation will happen
2. Who will live where, and when
3. Housing changes that will be made
4. Schooling changes that will be made
5. Other large changes that impact your child's day-to-day schedule

"I will emphasize again, you need to continue to tell the kids that they will now have two equivalent homes," Dr. Sheri says. "If this was set at the onset, it will help your discussions go more smoothly as time goes on."

Co-Parenting and Visitation

Dr. Sheri wisely explains that communication is the key to successful co-parenting. In this day and age, this doesn't have to mean the divorced couple needs to talk directly to each other. There are many apps and shared electronic calendars (such as Cozi and iCal) where scheduling can be shared and posted.

Gauge the developmental level of the kids to assess their level of understanding to help them adjust to the new schedule. Older kids can participate in shared electronic calendars, whereas younger children will need you both to guide their scheduled time.

Keep in mind that the kids need to continually get the message that they have two active, loving, parents. There is no primary or secondary parent. All you can do is set the expectations; you cannot control how the other parent acts and if they are going to follow the rules/guidelines. However, you can control how you act.

Valerie's ex wasn't quite getting the picture two years into being divorced that every time he "passed" on visitation with their son, it was affecting their child (not just her). Because he preferred to communicate via email and text, it was suggested she start color-coding a calendar with the dates and times when each parent had visitation. She decided to upload it to Dropbox, since her ex was down with technology, and seeing the facts would be the easiest way to share. Within a week of doing this, it became blaringly clear their 70/30 visitation schedule was actually more like an 85/15 schedule. He didn't miss a single scheduled date for a couple months after she started that system, and is now more mindful about making changes.

Holiday is a self-confessed bright color addict. So she naturally mapped out the month and color-coded about everything on a calendar she and her ex emailed to each other monthly regarding visitation schedules. Anytime a change was discussed, it was added to the calendar. He was happy to have her manage the calendar, and she was happy to use her favorite color: bright pink.

Transition Day

Tips for smooth transitions

Your first transition day will possibly be one of the hardest days during your entire divorce. You'll be on edge, and so will your ex as well as the children. Do your best to stay cool, calm, and collected. Put forth the brave face for the kids that this "new normal" is going to be okay. And if you're anything like us, save the breaking down for after the car pulls out of the driveway. Better yet, save it until it's out of the driveway and down the street, a good mile or two.

Once you have the first transition down, they will get easier for you, and hopefully for the children as well.

Dr. Sheri's best advice on transitions:

1. Give kids the space and time they need to adjust to the transition.
2. Assist the kids in acknowledging celebrations and holidays for the other parent.

She explains, "Help to make sure they get birthday presents, holiday presents, etc., for the other parent, so they are not left empty-handed or on their own. This is a little gesture that goes a long way. It is a terrible feeling for a kid to know it is dad's birthday, for example, but they are unable to get a present for dad."

Dr. Sheri adds, "I had a recent case where the dad and his new wife were having a baby. The ex-wife went out and got a present for the new baby. She brought both the son, as well as the present, to the hospital so that he could meet the new sibling. She even let him hold the new baby. Now that is extremely positive co-parenting. It took a lot of planning, discussion, and putting emotions aside to pull that off to make a smooth transition into being a brother for her son."

What NOT to do on transition day:

1. Don't quiz the kids about their time with the other parent or the other parent's life.
2. Don't assume that your ex is mistreating the kids.

"Do not accuse your ex of mistreatment just to get back at him," Dr. Sheri warns. "This will ultimately backfire and really upset your kids. Most importantly, it may turn them against you, as they will lose both confidence and trust in you."

This may be hard to do when your ex is more than two hours late and you have missed the hair appointment it took you over a month to get. Swallow the urge (later you can swallow the wine or whatever makes the bitter pill go down faster) to make defaming comments about their father, no matter how upset you are. You will only be hurting yourself in the long run.

In general, Dr. Sheri recommends that you "try your best to remain hyper-focused on what is best for the kids. Keep the balance on transition days so that your love for the kids is always higher and more of a priority than your hatred/resentment/anger for your ex. Do this regardless of why the marriage is breaking up or has broken up. Your kids did not ask for this, and they need to know it is okay to love both of their parents, as well as spend time with both of their parents."

"Continue to reassure the kids verbally and by example that you and your ex are going to work together on their behalf. Behave accordingly, regardless of what your ex does and how he acts."

Establish a Meeting Place

Handoffs are difficult for all parties involved, period. The one thing you can and should do is always establish a meeting place that will help avoid any confrontations during transitions.

If you know your children will cling to you like a kitten being declawed if you are anywhere near them during transitions, then pick somewhere like day care, or school, or a family member's house, where you won't need to be present. If your kids aren't clingy, but need the comfort of home for transitioning, then by all means plan to pick up and drop off at the house.

We both know from experience, establishing the regular meeting place for transition that best fits the needs of the children, right from the beginning, is one of the key elements to helping you both co-parent. This sets the tone for all future pickups and drop-offs.

If you agree to meet your ex halfway the first month, they will most likely expect you to keep doing this. If you allow your ex to constantly change times and places, he will most likely keep doing it. Your first few months of separation are just like your first few months of marriage: you are setting the tone for what to expect.

Be careful as to what you compromise on during transitions. Not only will this throw you off, but more importantly, it will throw your children off as well.

Packing for Transition Day

Do as much as you can to help the children gather their belongings before moving to and from the other parent's house. Again, they did not choose divorce, and packing (and ultimately remembering) all of their "things" is a chore no child should solely be responsible for.

This is especially true for younger children. If they forget their favorite stuffed animal, it may literally make them feel as if their world is upside down. Try to be sympathetic as well as realistic about how hard it is for your children to make actual transitions. A simple verbal (or written!) checklist may save tears as well as one of you the inevitable trip to pick up or deliver the aforementioned stuffed animal to your little one.

My eldest daughter had a complete breakdown once at age four, realizing she had left her favorite doll at daddy's house. As I listened to my daughter cry, I suddenly felt overwhelmed with guilt. This was not her fault. The fact that her daddy and I didn't live together was not her fault, yet she was paying the price right in that very moment. I called him and within thirty minutes she had her doll. Obviously, this may not always be possible, but as a parent I made the decision early on I would do anything I could to make sure the kids didn't suffer because of a choice I made.

—Holiday

Be forewarned, children may become resentful and angry, especially preteens and adolescents, when burdened with packing their things.

If they forget items they need for school, try to be understanding and lenient. Yes, your child should take some responsibility for ensuring they have everything they need for school no matter which home they are at. However, sometimes a book, or project, or report gets left at the other parent's house due to late nights or the sheer volume of course work your child is responsible for. Remember the big picture is helping them succeed, especially when it comes to school.

My ex forgot to repack my daughter's ballet shoes after picking her up at lessons almost every week. The first week, I lectured him when we didn't realize it until right before her second class. The second week it happened again, and this time I lectured her for not noticing until right before class again. I was not prepared for how upset this would make her (or me). The third week, I was already prepared with an extra set of ballet shoes ready to go. I accepted that this was just going to be one of the pitfalls of traveling back and forth between two homes, and I wasn't going to let frustrations from the situation get the best of me or her.

—Mary

What to Do When the Child Refuses to Go or Acts Out

Transitions become dreaded when a child refuses to go with the ex. Equally as hard is when you get the heartbreaking call from your child (or ex) for an early pickup or drop-off due to a meltdown. The selfish half of you is glad they want to be with you; however, the rational and good parent in you knows this is far from flattering and will only lead to more problems down the road if you don't set the example now.

Dr. Sheri says, "It is best to establish from the beginning that you and their father worked hard to create the schedule. Although you hear and understand your child is upset, and can acknowledge it, you both have confidence that with time and effort they will adjust. Do not allow the child to feel he/she has the power to change/manipulate the visits.

"If there is going to be trouble with being with the other parent, ideally the parents need to talk about this and come up with a plan of action to help the kids be more comfortable. Often this can include "transition objects" that the child needs to feel the presence of the other parent during the period of absence. Examples are pictures, clothing to wear, jewelry, a stuffed animal, and so on."

We know this may be hard to avoid or deal with if you and your ex are not on the best of terms. Asking your ex to show a picture of you or carry a stuffed animal everywhere they go if your child is prone to getting upset might go over like a box of rocks to the head. Gently, and in a non-lecturing kind of way, remind him it's is in the child's best interest to remain a united front as their parents, whether you are living together or not. Even if your ex doesn't want to do anything to help you in any way, they will normally certainly want to help their child.

Kids and Their "Stuff"

Warning: this will be an ongoing issue until your baby birdies have left the nest.

There are many things you can do to help manage/exchange your children's belongings. Consider this list the top advice we received from every divorced mother we interviewed, as well as ourselves. It will save you from many a headache and your child from many a meltdown.

- Have a complete set of personal hygiene items at each home—do not pack their toothbrush every time they visit daddy. You're just setting yourself up for failure if absolutely everything has to come back and forth.

- Allow children to bring their favorite toys/playthings with them between homes (within reason). Tossing a few stuffed animals in their bag should be permitted, but the Barbie Dream House needs to stay put.
- Both parents should have complete wardrobes for the children. They should never feel like they are living out of a suitcase or don't fully reside at one of the homes. A proper closet/dresser, etc. should be established for each child in their bedroom at each home. Complete wardrobes include shoes, uniforms, and inexpensive sports gear.
- Have two of their absolute favorite things. If they just can't live without Freddy the Bear, then have his identical twin, Teddy the Bear, at the other house. If their sparkly red shoes are in high rotation, have the same pair at both houses.

Remember when you cried for hours on end when you were a child and left your sticker book at your best friend's house? The stuff your children love is no different. You were panicked that you might never get it back, as well as sad you didn't have something you truly loved and cared for in your hands. Bring back that feeling you had as a child and channel it when you have to drive thirty minutes each way to retrieve their One Direction covered notebook with all their drawings in it, because they will "just die" if they can't have it to doodle in today.

Consistent Routine

Children thrive with a routine. This is not a secret. Chances are you probably thrive from routines yourself! The one thing we do know about routines is that they must be consistent and predictable in order for children to feel comfortable.

To help you set and follow a routine, we suggest the following:

- Minimize changes in schedules, routines, and transitions.
- If you have to travel for your job, make sure your child stays with the other parent or same caregiver each time you are gone.
- Find a routine that works for you; every family is different.

Dr. Sheri notes, "Kids will eventually adjust to their new reality, whatever that reality is. If your ex does in fact have to cancel or skip their planned visitation, do not overly nag the other parent. Do not put down that parent in front of the kids.

"Do reassure the kids that it is okay to talk with you about their feelings, but be careful to not impose your feelings into the situation. Air those out with your own adult support system so your negative feelings (which you are allowed to have) do not become your children's burden.

"Do stay consistent yourself; no matter what your ex chooses to do. Your kids will see this and it will help them feel secure with you."

> *My ex pretty much let our son set his own bedtime, despite his age, and despite me telling him our son was always a total mess the day after drop off. It wasn't until formal schooling that the teachers also started noticing a big difference on certain days (days after our son spent the night with him!). Thank goodness it was finally someone besides me telling my ex how important it was he ensured that our son stick to a set schedule.*
>
> —Valerie

Schooling/Education

Schooling and education are probably one of the main focuses for not only you and your ex, but also your children. It is their every day, and the vast majority of their life. With that being said, we know how important it is to maintain normalcy in your child's school life during a divorce.

"It is okay to let the school counselor and teachers know that the kids are going through life transitions," says Dr. Sheri. "Ask them to alert you if there are any changes and/or concerns academically, behaviorally, and socially.

"Most teachers these days communicate with parents via email; make sure all parenting figures are on the teachers' email distribution list. It is a burden to teachers to have to spend extra time to respond to parents about school assignments and activities because divorced parents won't talk with each other. Like with the kids, it is not the teachers' fault or responsibility because the students' parents are no longer together.

"As a general rule of thumb, it is ideal for the parents to be co-parenting well with respect to the kids' schooling. It should be a goal that the teacher is unaware of it as an issue and has no extra work or concerns about the student as a result.

"Many schools have counseling groups available for students who are going through divorce in their families. These groups could be helpful for kids but are not needed for all; it really depends on how the kids are adjusting and how the parents are behaving.

"Ideally, both parents should participate in kids' school (and extracurricular) activities.

This means, for example:

- Having the teacher email you both (as described above)
- Going to student-teacher conferences together
- Alternate going on field trips
- Both parents attending special performances, presentations, awards, etc.

"Try your best to leave negative emotions aside and be there to support and celebrate your kids," Dr. Sheri advises. "It is helpful, if at all possible, to sit close enough to your ex during these special moments for your children's benefit. This is so your kids can see you in one eyeshot instead of having to scan the room in two different places to find their parents. I cannot emphasize enough how much anxiety it creates in kids when they know their parents' negative emotions for each other are spilling out into their school environment."

Adolescents and Teenagers (*A whole different ball game*)

Adolescence is typically a time when you're racking your brain on how to best deal with teenagers and their raging hormones, need to be independent, and sassy attitudes. Add a divorce to the equation and undoubtedly one of you will end up wanting to pull your hair out—or paint it blue.

Dr. Sheri's best advice if you're dealing with teenagers is to keep marital and divorce business personal and private. "Do not lean on your teen as a friend or confidante. That is inappropriate, too much pressure, and sets up an imbalance that often backfires where the teen eventually resents you," she explains.

In addition, she says, "Do not talk with your teens about laws. Never offer them the knowledge that when they get to a certain age, they can choose who they want to be with."

At the age of twelve, my eldest son told me his dad had informed him that as soon as he was fourteen he could choose to go live with him. I told him his dad was mistaken. One minute later my son came towards me, laptop open, with his googled results showing, trying to prove me wrong. I couldn't believe that my ex would ever threaten disrupting a living situation that was working and was best for our son. I still don't believe that he was the one that told him. I shut my son's computer screen, walked away from my son without saying a word, and slowly walked into my bedroom where I shut the door and sat on my bed in shock for a good hour or so. I think it was in that very moment I realized I no longer had my little boy, I had a full-blown teenager on my hands.

—Shelly

"Along the same lines, do not bring your kids to your lawyer's office and make them feel pressured to sign a letter of election." Dr. Sheri warns. "Remember, you have told your kids they should love you both and not have to choose loyalties."

She adds, "Be especially aware of if/when the teen is trying to manipulate you or play one parent against the other. Teens are infamous for this, and parents need to work particularly hard as co-parents during this time and phase of life."

Dating and Introducing Children

This is probably the second hottest topic when it comes to kids and divorce. You will most likely find yourself swimming in the dating pool sometime during and/or after your divorce. With so many different pressures on you, as both a single woman as well as a newly single mother, it's only natural to be overwhelmed by the many suggestions out there on how to handle dating with children.

Which guideposts do you follow?

Let us rephrase that. Which guideposts do you follow so you can successfully play the role of both caring girlfriend and stellar mother?

To help cut down on the confusion, Dr. Sheri has developed a list:

The General Rules of Thumb for Dating and Introducing Your New Partner to the Children:

- No introductions of another partner for a minimum of a year after the finalization of the divorce; this is easier said than done.
- Only introduce another partner IF the relationship seems like it will be serious and potentially long term.
- Do not force the relationship on the kids. It needs to grow over time.
- Balance time with the kids, so it doesn't appear to the kids that the new relationship is more important than they are.
- Reassure the kids that a potential future partner does not mean that you're replacing their father in any way.

Follow these suggestions from Dr. Sheri and you won't be regretting a relationship that doesn't work out. We suggest showing your kids with your actions and attention that no matter what the future brings with your partner, they are and always will be the most important thing to you.

Fighting with Your Ex

As we and Dr. Sheri have said more than a few times, your child did not choose for his parents to get divorced. Regardless of the circumstances, children should never have to witness their parents' disagreements, especially when the argument is related to the child—ever.

A fight with your ex over money, schedules, visitations, etc., is inevitable. Doing it in front of your kids is not.

Dr. Sheri states, "Your child should never feel caught in the middle between mom and dad." We couldn't agree more. Bottom line: don't do it. Not to them, not to your ex, not even to yourself.

Even when your ex is teeing you up, and hoping you take the swing while the kids are within eyeshot and/or earshot, take the pass. Once they are safely away from you feel free to lose your s#%@—big time. (Remember that voodoo doll we spoke about in earlier chapters?) Just don't ever take the bait or be the one holding the fishing pole when it comes to fighting in front of the kids.

You're not only setting an example of how adults should behave and cooperate, you're also showing your children how you expect them to handle themselves now and in the future.

> *Every time I had to see my ex he would take a jab at me. The kind of jab the kids didn't realize was a slap in the face, but intended to get a big reaction out of me in front of our kids. I literally would have to physically pinch myself to remind myself that this is exactly what he wanted, and a better win for me was just to smile and pretend I didn't care what he was talking about for our kids' sake.*
>
> —Melody

The Importance of Co-parenting

(Dr. Sheri's final piece of advice)

"Overall, you and your ex have control over how well, or poorly, your kids do with the divorce. As a general rule, from what I've seen over the years, the more the parents maintain their battle with each other through the kids post-divorce, the worse the long-term prognosis is for the kids. Try not to let this happen to you and your children," Dr. Sheri advises.

"I tell parents all the time to love their kids more than they hate/resent each other. Obviously, in an emotionally charged situation like a divorce, this is easier said than done." She adds, "I am aware that many situations are less than ideal, and that there are no cookie cutter, perfect situations. However, the ideal situation is, and always will be, both parents working together on behalf of their kids."

The Main Goal

Make sure your children feel safe and loved.

Books

Find books that normalize the experience and treat divorce as the life transition that it is. There are many specialty books for specific situations, such as when the other parent is absent or when other family members, such as grandparents, are raising the child. Children's books offer a safe place to open the door for healthy conversations and also show children that they aren't alone in this process. Seek out the right books for your particular situation. The books below are general books that should help in almost any situation where children are involved.

Suggested reading for parents:

- *The Truth About Children and Divorce*, Robert E. Emery, PhD
- *Helping Your Kids Cope with Divorce the Sandcastles Way*, M. Gary Neuman
- *Putting Children First*, JoAnne Pedro-Carroll

Suggested reading for children:

- *Two Homes*, Claire Masurel
- *Standing on My Own Two Feet*, Tamara Schmitz
- *It's Not Your Fault, Koko Bear*, Vicki Lansky

Suggested reading for teens:

- *Now What Do I Do?*, Lynn Cassella-Kapusinski
- *The Big D; Divorce Thru the Eyes of a Teen*, Krista Smith
- *The Divorce Helpbook for Teens*, Cynthia MacGregor

Get Off the Boat
{settlement options}

Disclaimer: Divorce laws differ from state to state. Please refer to your professional counsel for specific laws regarding your personal legal circumstances and divorce. This chapter is meant to provide a general breakdown of common divorce settlements and questions pertaining to such.

"All's fair in love and war."

—Anonymous

If only this were true.

If we could put divorce in a pretty box and label it "one size fits all," we would. But the truth is all divorces are different. The same goes for the settlement options and outcomes. There are multiple factors to consider when settlement options are presented. The most common question asked is, "Is this fair?"

The definition of a "fair" settlement will certainly vary between parties, so it's nearly impossible to define a fair settlement. We can, however, help you prioritize your options and outline some basic guidelines you should stick to.

When it comes to divorce settlements, there are three main issues to resolve:

1. Custody of minor children
2. Alimony and child support
3. Division of marital property

Top questions you (and everyone else getting divorced) are probably thinking that pertain to all three main issues:

- What are my legal rights?
- How much child support will I get?
- Will I get custody of the kids?
- Will he have to pay me alimony?
- Can I keep the house and my car?

These big questions are probably keeping you up late at night. Typically, these concerns are discussed during the initial meeting with your attorney. While your attorney won't be able to answer them on the spot, he/she should be able to assess your marital circumstances and give you a general idea of what you can expect. This is why it's crucial to choose an attorney who can work through these financial details and thoroughly explore all options, as was discussed in Chapter 7, "Oh Captain, My Captain." Your financial future is at stake, and you don't want to be left in the poorhouse while your ex is enjoying a financially secure lifestyle in the penthouse.

Your final settlement will be a work in progress. Do not rush the process. Patience is key.

Holiday will never forget the conversation she had with her dad a few months into the divorce process.

Holiday: "Dad, I just want this to be over!"

Dad: "Holiday, take it easy. Calm down. Be patient. He wants you to give in and give up. Just like the early bird gets the worm, the patient one gets the reward. There is no timeline on divorce. Sit on it. Pray on it. Let time take its course. See what he says, and wait for him to get anxious. He will, but it's going to take some time. And, did I mention patience?"

> *My father's famous words. Patience, darling. Patience. If there's one thing I'm really not good at, it's being patient. I learned at a young age not to pray for patience, because sure enough, God will test you, and a test on patience is never fun.*
>
> —Holiday

While you're patiently preparing for this settlement process, your brain will be filled with concerns and unanswered questions. Your attorney will be able to provide you with some answers based on your personal situation, but like anything, there are several mistakes to look out for during this process. Take our advice and avoid them.

Don't Get Screwed

The top five mistakes women make in divorce settlements:

1. Not knowing the value of your assets and trusting your spouse when he says you already know everything.
2. Forgetting about Uncle Sam—the IRS wants your money, honey, regardless of your marital status.
3. Failure to budget properly and plan accurately for your future.
4. Ignoring debt and your credit score.
5. Not understanding retirement accounts and their value.

I wasn't focused completely on the most important aspects of the divorce settlement: financial matters. I was worried about not spending every day with my son. I was worried about having to give up the house I brought my baby home to. I was worried that if I didn't hurry up, the divorce would never happen and I would have to remain sad for the rest of my life. Not that these weren't important things, they were just the wrong things to worry about—they are the things that normally work themselves out. The financial stuff . . . that's the stuff that will haunt you for years.

—Valerie

Custody Arrangements

"Will I get custody?"

When it comes to custody, the judge will ask questions regarding what custody arrangement will be "in the best interest" of the children. There are multiple factors to consider, such as the age of children, personal relationships with each parent, siblings, school, other family, work schedules, etc. Depending on who is filing for divorce, your custody situation may vary. It takes quite a lot for a court to strip a mother of her parental rights. More often than not, the mother will be awarded primary physical custody with a percentage split given to the father.

Multiple factors come into play when deciding on a custody arrangement. Ultimately, you'll have to figure out what works best for you, your ex, and, most of all, your kids. We'll give you a breakdown of the most common custody arrangements found today in divorce settlements. We'll also give you our two cents on what we really think (warning: our filter is about to go out the window).

Before you consider any custody arrangement, it is important for you and your ex to discuss any and all of the factors below. This will give you a true snapshot of what the most realistic and beneficial arrangement is not only for the kids, but for what your capabilities are and will be.

Your top priority is the present and future needs of children. Here are some things to consider:

- The age of your children
- The developing needs of your children (the social calendar of a middle school girl is much different than a toddler's social schedule)
- The current and future school track they are enrolled in (gifted classes, IEPs, etc.)
- The special needs of your children, such as medical needs, special schools, and extracurricular commitments
- Geography—what if one of you decides to move?

We recommend reading this list with your ex, as if it affects both of you on an equal level. But, if we're being honest here, as the mother you're normally left to pick up the slack. So, (start reading to him now) how will you and your ex agree to handle ***when***:

- a child is sick and it's during your scheduled parenting time;
- multiple siblings have to be in multiple places at the same time;
- one of you has to work late;
- your child has an appointment (doctor, haircut, etc.);
- school-related issues come up
  - school emergencies (little Suzie busted her chin during recess)
  - parent–teacher conferences
  - open house/meet the teacher days
  - discipline/behavior problems during school
  - early release days

    - snow days
    - teacher in-service days
    - managing homework
- school projects (There's nothing better than a kid coming back to your house only to find out a school project was due that the other parent didn't take care of during their time.);
- it's summer (What will happen with the kids when school is out?);
- there are special events like birthday parties (who is responsible for purchasing the gifts), fall festivals, dance recitals, sports games, family commitments, etc., that fall on your time;
- there are extracurricular activities (If Noah's baseball practice is every Monday, Wednesday, and Friday from 4:30 to 5:30 p.m., the parent who has designated custody will be expected to take him to practice during those times or be responsible for finding a way to get Noah to practice if there is a work commitment); or
- one parent wants to keep coaching, say, your son's travel baseball team (basically taking up every weekend for five months of the year), which will result in your daughter sacrificing her weekend time with "the coach" when she is dragged to the baseball field or pawned off on a friend/family member or anyone willing to take care of her.

The list could go on and on, trust us! But you get the drift. These are the kind of things that are best talked about whether your child is two or twelve. Before deciding any custody plan, each parent must be clear about the reality of their day-to-day situation in order for your visitation to truly work.

You may be incapable of being honest to each other, but at least be honest for the sake of your children and the potential of letting them down about your true capabilities.

For us, the responsibility of getting kids to practices, rehearsals, games, etc., has mostly fallen on us. Whether it's their father's scheduled time or not, we know this is how it's going to be. It's part of the gig, and we're okay with it. You have to think about the circumstances for your family and figure out what will work best for all of you, especially if you both work full-time jobs. Does it mean it's easy for us or necessarily fair that if our children are home sick it always falls on us? Absolutely not. But, like we said before, the kids didn't ask for a divorce, and they need their mommy to love on them when they are sick.

My girls shouldn't have to miss out on things like playing sports, attending birthday parties, special weekend activities, etc., just because their father and I can't agree on who covers what or a definite schedule.

—Holiday

50/50 Split

A typical 50/50 custody schedule would look like this:

SUN	MON	TUES	WED	THUR	FRI	SAT
YOU	EX	EX	EX	EX	EX	EX
EX	YOU	YOU	YOU	YOU	YOU	YOU
YOU	EX	EX	EX	EX	EX	EX
EX	YOU	YOU	YOU	YOU	YOU	YOU

It looks like the perfect solution, right? Think again.

We're going to be bold here and just come right out with it. Too many parents live in dreamland, believing their children's lives will be perfectly balanced and have minimal disruption with an equal custody arrangement. We couldn't disagree more, unless you have extreme extenuating circumstances, like a job that requires frequent out-of-town travel or physical limitations.

Holiday and her ex originally agreed on this option until her attorney advised her against it. It wasn't because her ex was a bad father, or incapable; it was simply in the best interest of the children.

We were both heartbroken when we filed for divorce, but my ex's only plea was for us to agree on 50/50 custody. I was experiencing so much guilt, and I truly believed it would be best for our kids to see both of us equally. The children weren't the ones asking for divorce, and he was a good dad. As far as I was concerned, they loved their daddy and deserved to see him as much as they saw me, regardless of our marital status.

When I met with my attorney, I immediately told her we had agreed on 50/50. She dropped her reading glasses to the edge of her nose and shook her head. Her words of wisdom spoke volumes to me, especially after I had experienced divorce within my own family as a teenager. She told me the children needed a stable home, and by floating back and forth between houses they would never have a "home base." As a mother I could understand that, but why did it sound so bad?

My attorney showed me the calendar of a 60/40 split, and I realized the breakdown was much more promising than I had thought in my head. The truth was clear: as their mother, I took care of almost everything pertaining to the children. I scheduled their doctor's appointments, arranged extracurricular activities, attended school conferences, stayed home with them when they were sick, and pretty much everything in between. As a self-employed, work-from-home mom, I was able to have flexibility as a parent, whereas their dad had a very demanding job and work schedule. The reality was he would never be able to legitimately pull his weight as a 50/50 dad. There was just no way. I knew my attorney was right. I presented him with the 60/40 split, and after talking through it he agreed. It just made sense.

—Holiday

Why 50/50 Rarely Works

While it sounds like a perfect solution, it usually results in one of two scenarios:

1. an expensive visit back to court for custody modification

or

2. a really pissed off ex-wife who is constantly picking up the slack of her ex (we've met way too many)

There are several different ways families break up the 50/50 visitation split, the most common being one week on, one week off, with the children rotating houses each week. The problem with this is that the children never truly get "settled."

Think of yourself on vacation. You arrive at your destination, unpack your suitcase, and as soon as you start to feel settled, it's time to pack up and go home.

Now, imagine you're not even going somewhere fun, like Mexico, you're just going between mom's house and dad's house.

As a kid, floating back and forth between mom's house and dad's house can become really annoying. It's also hard work, especially as the kids get older and have to start keeping up with their stuff. All it takes is one meltdown from a teenage daughter who doesn't have the "right" pair of jeans at mom's house because she forgot to bring them from dad's house last week. With younger kids a 50/50 split might be easier at first, but as the kids get older it's almost impossible to keep a healthy, balanced lifestyle.

Forget about the "stuff." Let's get to the real problem with equally shared custody.

One of the biggest challenges women face with 50/50 custody is the father's ability to equally contribute and, ultimately, be responsible for everything that happens during his 50 percent of the time. No matter how hard they try, it honestly just doesn't cut it in the long run.

Let's take a classmate's birthday party for example, which would include purchasing and wrapping a gift, dropping your child off at the party, killing most of the day while your child plays in a huge monkey-shaped jump house with duct tape all over it and eats cake filled with high fructose corn syrup, then picking your child up. While this isn't a totally impossible feat for a dad, we are saying that it is rare that they're up for everything it entails.

A 50/50 split of time is doable, but a 50/50 split of parental responsibilities is nearly impossible.

In fact, we're pretty sure if you showed him the list we gave before as well as the birthday party scenario (because, guess what, he hasn't thought of any of this because up until now you have done it all!) he would just reply, "Umm." He won't figure it out, he won't know what to do, and he won't have a backup plan. Not because he isn't a good dad, not because he's not willing to give it the old college try, but because he's a man. He doesn't have the maternal gene, and the bottom line is this: he is not their mother.

The Ex-Wives' Advice:

Don't agree to a 50/50 custody arrangement (which will also affect your child support) unless you truly believe your soon-to-be ex will be able to fulfill his 50 percent of parental duties during his time with the children. Again, maybe you have to travel every other week for work or have physical limitations, so 50/50 is perfect. Or maybe your ex has been and will continue to be a stay-at-home dad while you focus on work and bringing home the bacon, whether you're married or not. We're not saying this never works. However, for the typical family it just doesn't. We don't want to see you in a constant battle with your ex, or your children, on what will always be most likely a difficult situation for all of you.

60/40 Split

As we mentioned, Holiday and her ex settled on a 60/40 custody arrangement. Their schedule was as follows:

SUN	MON	TUES	WED	THUR	FRI	SAT
EX	EX	HOL	HOL	HOL	HOL	HOL
HOL	EX	HOL	HOL	EX	EX	EX
EX	EX	HOL	HOL	HOL	HOL	HOL
HOL	EX	HOL	HOL	EX	EX	EX

Holiday had roughly seventeen days a month and her ex had eleven. During this time, she and her ex lived within ten miles of each other, and the children were ages two and four. You will notice that her ex had the kids every Monday night, and Holiday had the kids every Tuesday and Wednesday night. This made scheduling for play dates, extracurricular activities, etc., much easier. Holiday knew she would be able to take the girls to a dance class every Tuesday, gymnastics on Wednesdays, etc.

The schedule was predictable; the kids knew they were with mommy mostly during the week, and they also knew Monday nights were their special nights with daddy, no matter what. Monday nights were a night "off" for Holiday. The perfect time to meet a friend for dinner, catch up on laundry, take a class, or go on a date. Yes, dating did eventually enter the picture, and it will for you, too; yet another reason to have a solid schedule in place for both you and your kids.

After three years of this schedule, Holiday got remarried and moved twenty-seven miles away from her ex. Their schedule had shifted, and they have had some bumps in the road. But again, Holiday is the mother, and she has the majority of custody, so this also gave her more control when making the decision to move. Had she been bound to a 50/50 custody arrangement, it would have been almost impossible for her to manage moving thirty-five minutes away from her ex. It would have made driving back and forth to school an absolute nightmare for the kids, and the extracurricular activities would have to have been located somewhere in the middle. Not. Gonna. Happen.

How 60/40 Can Work for You

A 60/40 schedule gives you some freedom and flexibility as a parent, but also provides enough time for the children to continue to build strong relationships with both parents while living in two homes. From our research (and Holiday's experience) a 60/40 split usually works best when:

- both parents are able to contribute significantly to time and parental responsibilities, but one parent will be taking the lead;
- you are flexible and willing to accommodate each other should a change in schedule arise;
- you and your soon-to-be ex are able to communicate effectively and co-parent without fighting about the schedule;
- your children feel comfortable with the schedule and feel safe and loved at both homes; and
- both homes will be relatively close to each other (within reason for school, friends, extracurricular activities, etc.)

70/30 or 75/25 Split

This is probably one of the most popular and widely used custody plans American families use. This is the plan Valerie and her ex settled on, a 70/30 custody arrangement. Their schedule is as follows:

SUN	MON	TUES	WED	THUR	FRI	SAT
EX	V	V	EX	V	V	V
V	V	V	EX	V	EX	EX
EX	V	V	EX	V	V	V
V	V	V	EX	V	EX	EX

Valerie had her son roughly twenty days a month, and her ex had him ten. During this time, she and her ex lived within fifteen miles of each other and their son was three years old. You will notice that her ex has their son every Wednesday night, and Valerie has him the remaining weeknights. This made scheduling for play dates, extracurricular activities, etc., much, much (much) easier.

Valerie and her son's schedule is very predictable. She has the ability to pretty much plan her son's schedule and run with it. Her son knew he had a "Daddy Day," as he called it, one night a week, and looked forward to that special time with him. Valerie knew she had at least one night a week to recoup from the demands of being a single parent, and looked equally as forward to what she called her "Off Night." She knew she could eat popcorn for dinner (as the main and only course), or meet a group of friends for dinner, or go on a date here or there, or just catch up on sleep.

Having every other weekend off was also a great balance and allowed her to get out and do things she normally couldn't do while taking care of her son. It was the little things, like being able to sleep in past 7:00 a.m., that helped fill her tank back up.

Valerie is mostly happy with this plan, but she was not happy that her ex kept their son on Sunday night and dropped him back off directly at school Monday morning. She felt their young son needed a reset of sorts on Sunday night to get ready for school. But she and her ex were anything but amiable during their divorce. If that meant she rarely had to see her ex by him picking up and dropping off their son either directly at school or with an after-school sitter, well, she considered it a very small sacrifice. As their son gets older and his school commitments and obligations get larger, this might have to change. But for now it works and has helped Valerie's ex drop the sword he mostly wielded during their divorce.

How 70/30 or 75/25 Can Work for You

The common 70/30 or 75/25 schedule gives you some freedom and flexibility as the primary parent and also provides enough time for the children to continue to build strong relationships with both parents while living in two homes. From our research (and Valerie's experience) a 70/30 or 75/25 split usually works best when:

- the primary parent is able to contribute significantly to time and parental responsibilities, but the other parent will be taking the "backup" position if needed;
- you understand that as the primary parent you must be flexible and willing to accommodate each other should a change in schedule arise;
- you and your soon-to-be ex prefer to keep communication centered on your children and co-parent without fighting about the schedule due to the larger amount of time spent with the primary parent;
- your children feel comfortable with the schedule and feel safe and loved at both homes. It might mean missing some social events, but due to the majority of the week being spent at one house, it's normally not a problem;
- both homes ideally will be relatively close to each other (within reason for school, friends, extracurricular activities, etc.); and
- one of the parents has a larger role at work and would rather devote their entire weekend to the child, as opposed to leaving them with sitters or other family members during the week.

No matter which custody or visitation plan you and your ex agree on, it is important for us to remind you that your ex might not always take the children during their scheduled time with them. Yes, despite it being scheduled, and despite it being outlined in a legally binding document, it's best for you to be mentally prepared in case this happens.

Valerie can attest to this. There were numerous times her ex would tell her at the last minute that he would not be taking their son, and sometimes for extended periods of time. Additionally, much of the holiday and vacation time he fought her for during the divorce went mostly unused, and it was up to her to cover that time.

Getting extra time with her son was awesome; however, this made it hard for her to ever make plans that she could keep. In order to cover the scheduled times her ex decided he wasn't going to take their son, she had to cancel plans as well as modify/cancel trips she had already paid for. This drove her bananas, and many times she wondered if she would ever have a social or dating life again. To add insult to injury, any time she had to cover her ex's time or modify her plans in order to do so, it cost her even more money (babysitters, food, activities, canceled flights, etc.) she didn't have with her already tight budget. This drove her even more bananas (more like f'ing crazy).

Our **strong suggestion** is to include verbiage in your separation agreement stating that if the party who has scheduled visitation time cancels without an extenuating circumstance, a specific financial amount will be paid to the parent that will have the children. This amount will be used to cover the additional expenses, such as babysitters, nonrefundable deposits paid for canceled trips, extra costs incurred if the children join you for an activity or trip. You and your attorney should discuss this to determine what would be fair.

Once your ex has to pay anywhere from twenty dollars to two thousand dollars for passing on scheduled visitation, he's more likely to think twice before canceling again.

This is especially important if you have a job that requires you to work on the weekends. If your ex does not take advantage of his scheduled visitation time, you might find yourself in a horrible predicament. Make sure you always have a backup plan.

It should also be noted that most of the time the two of you will know in advance if something will throw off scheduled visitation time with the kiddos. It can be anything from a family wedding to a work trip or relatives visiting. These are times you should work with your ex (and your ex should work with you!) on covering for each other. It is common to trade weekends on the rare occasion when these types of things happen, and you should be open to doing what is best for the children.

How Much Child Support Will I Get?

The question heard 'round the globe. This is the first and foremost question almost every woman will ask herself (as well as everyone she knows who is divorced). Or, if she is the breadwinner, she will ask, "How much child support will I have to pay?" All states are required to have minimum child support guidelines. Your attorney will provide you with a child support worksheet, and there are several factors added into the calculation. This is not the time to be lazy! Break out your budget worksheet and get to work! Every single expense needs to be documented and accounted for, otherwise you'll get stuck paying for things while your ex-husband enjoys his fancy car and fine wine. Be diligent about submitting the proper information to ensure your child support is what will be necessary to support your family now, as well as in the future.

This is where your divorce financial planner we discussed in Chapter 6, "Choose Your Crew," will come in handy. Your financial needs with young children are much different than they are with teenagers. It is crucial to plan properly and project future expenses and make adjustments as necessary.

Legally we can't give you specific numbers when it comes to child support, but here are the main factors that go into the calculation:

- Gross monthly income of the noncustodial parent
- Gross monthly income of the custodial parent
- Number of children
- Cost of living/family expenses
- Cost of family group health insurance
- Who pays for family group health insurance
- Amount of time each parent spends with children (refer back to the 50/50, 60/40, 70/30, and 75/25 plans discussed previously)

Modifying Your Custody Arrangement

Some people have asked me if we went back to court for adjustments in child support or for legal documentation of our schedule change once I got remarried and our visitation schedule had to change. The answer is no. Why? Because, thankfully, he and I were and still are able to work together in an effective manner to do what's best for the kids. We both have their best interest at heart. It's how we do things, and it's how our family works.

As far as child support goes, either of us could request a modification at any time, but again, we are able to work together effectively to make things work. If we headed back to court, could it possibly result in more child support from my ex? Sure. But it would also cost me a fortune (and a headache) to gather all of the documents necessary to proceed. There are two sides to the child support coin given our personal circumstances:

1. *Technically, we aren't 60/40 anymore (honestly it's more like 80/20 now that I've moved).*
2. *My income (down), cost of living (down), expenses (down), etc., have changed over the past few years.*

I've also noticed that my ex's lifestyle seems to have bumped up a notch. My guess is he's making more money now than he ever has, and is probably planning a kickass vacation to Bora Bora with his new wife. Could I take him back to court and demand proof of his income, provide the court with proof of his drastic decrease in parenting time, and request a modification of child support? You bet. Will I do it? Not unless I absolutely have to.

—Holiday

Most people try to avoid modification unless they really have no alternative. They especially like to avoid it when it comes to visitation, as children's needs change every year and your settlement agreement should include verbiage stating that both parties will be sensitive and acknowledge this. Hopefully you are in a situation like Holiday and her ex, where they are amiable and seem to keep their eye on the prize: making sure their girls are happy, healthy, and feel loved. But if you're not, please know you are not alone.

The realities of modification are that it is extremely expensive and very time-consuming. Imagine having to compile all of the same paperwork you just spent hours and days and weeks compiling for your divorce all over again. And this time for just one particular issue. If you're going to go through the extensive effort needed for a modification, it better be worth it, and not just because Wednesday nights don't work for you anymore because of tennis team.

When it comes to modifications in visitation or custody, you must pretty much prove two things:

1. The children's needs have changed significantly, and the current plan is not adequately meeting them.

and/or

2. One of the parent's visitation hours, capabilities, or limitations is affecting your children (such as a move, a new demanding job, or, God forbid, an addiction problem) and has changed the overall picture significantly.

Notice we keep saying *significantly* here. Complaining to a judge that your ex is supposed to have your kiddos 25 percent of the time but only takes them 21 percent of the time is not going to hold much weight. However, proving he is supposed to have them 30 percent of the time but only takes them 10 to 16 percent of the time is something to consider modifying and would most likely entitle you to more support if deemed a valid request worth modifying.

What if He Doesn't Pay?

In a perfect world, people would pay their bills on time and fulfill their obligations to society. Unfortunately, this isn't always the case, especially when it comes to divorce. If your ex-husband refuses to pay your child support (or is not paying you on time, the correct amount, etc.), you need to take action immediately. Hopefully this won't happen to you, but just to be on the safe side, we want you to know how important it is for you to take action now and not wait.

There are laws in effect designed to protect women (and specifically children) from a parent who is withholding support. RUN, don't walk, to your nearest child support office and fill out the paperwork you need to start your case. Like anything else in the legal world, this will take time. So the faster you start the process, the faster you'll get your money. The courts will start an investigation, and you will need to provide proof to back up your claim (just another reason to keep all of your paperwork, checking accounts, checks received, receipts, etc., organized).

If the court is able to determine that your ex is, in fact, delinquent with his payments, or in violation of his court-ordered child support obligation, he will be charged with contempt of court. This is serious business and isn't to be taken lightly.

Far too many women have to fight through this process, so we want you to be as emotionally prepared as possible. When you take child support through the state legal system, chances are your ex will get angry. Very, very angry. He may even threaten you with continuing to hold out on paying you. Don't allow his threats to interfere with what is legally yours!

Stay strong and keep those big girl panties on—you need to protect yourself and, most of all, your children!

Perhaps you and your soon-to-be ex are on friendly, cordial terms, and you trust he will give you a check every week for what you are legally entitled to. Try it out and see how that goes. Different couples manage child support differently. Holiday's ex usually writes her a check every other week. She keeps track of the checks being deposited and sends him friendly reminders anytime it's past due. They are not the norm, nor is it recommended to exchange money this way. By sending her ex reminders and requests for money owed to her, it places him in a position of power. This isn't exactly ideal if you aren't on good terms, and even if you are, it could potentially cause uncomfortable situations.

Valerie has found the best way for her to ensure child support is paid in full and on time is to have it deducted from her ex's paychecks. This also eliminates the need for a conversation and/or verbal exchange when giving money. It requires minimal reminders to the ex, and that's a good thing in her situation (for both of them actually).

There is a certain amount of a power a man feels when he hands a check to a woman. Subliminally, it may be best for you to make arrangements for your support to be paid via electronic transfer. That way there is no room for negotiation or for feeling vulnerable when exchanging children and checks.

Do not make the same mistake Kim did . . .

When my ex and I filed for divorce, we both agreed we didn't want things to get ugly. We didn't want to drain our life's savings on attorney fees to fight about things we thought we could handle on our own. We had been married fourteen years, and we had drifted apart. We didn't love each other anymore, and the decision to divorce was mutual. We had two children (ages five and nine), and both of us worked demanding full-time jobs with hefty salaries. Our income was almost the same, but when we got divorced I stayed in the house with the boys, and my ex moved to a small apartment. We agreed on 60/40 custody, and when it came to child support totals, my monthly support didn't allot too much money.

I also sadly didn't prepare properly or project the expenses from staying in our big house and being the primary custodial parent. My attorney brought this to our attention during mediation, and my ex made the statement, "I don't want to fight about money. How about I just give you whatever extra money you need each month and then we won't have to waste any more time in this court? You know I'm a good man and a good dad, hell, I'll never let you live like dirt. You know I will always take care of you and make sure you and the kids have whatever you need." And just like that I agreed. I trusted him, and, honestly, I think he truly believed what he was saying. I think we both wanted to believe what he said, that he would always take care of us.

The ugly truth came a few months later, when the air conditioner broke in our three-story home. The bill was more than eighteen hundred dollars, and I was left worrying about paying the mortgage. Here's where the problem started: I didn't want to have to ask him for money. I didn't want to feel like I would owe him something, and I didn't want to give him leverage over me in any way. But I didn't have a choice. I couldn't pay the bill. I finally sucked up my pride and asked him for the extra money to cover the bill, and his response was, "Why don't you ask your boyfriend?" I didn't have a boyfriend at the time; in fact, I wasn't even dating. But he was going through the anger phase of grief (perfect timing, really), and just assumed I had been dating someone. What should have been a decent conversation after our little agreement in the mediation room turned into something ugly. And I mean ugly.

I was bitter, resentful, and angry at him for making me feel guilty. He made me feel ashamed for asking him for the money that should have been rightfully mine to begin with. Had our child support payments been reconfigured with accurate numbers, it would have provided me with enough cushion to budget for emergency expenses.

But I trusted him in my moment of weakness and was burned in return.

What's the moral of the story? Get it in writing. Don't accept his promises when he promises to "give you extra money if you need it." Promises made verbally in the mediation room don't hold any weight out of or back in court. And, unfortunately, that's where we ended up. After almost a year of reworking our financials, I am finally receiving the child support that I should have fought for to begin with. I share this story with you, because if it helps one woman get the settlement she is entitled to, then my mistake was worthwhile.

—Kim

Modifying Child Support

Things change over time, and your financial situation now may be drastically different from what it is five, ten, or fifteen years from now. (For some of us that are self-employed that is more like five, ten, or fifteen minutes from now!)

When I got divorced, my kids were one, three, and six, so our extracurricular expenses were minimal. Fast-forward ten years and it's a different ball game. Extracurricular activities, summer camps, transportation costs. (You're not getting away with a little dance class at your neighborhood studio anymore; by the time they're ten you'll be driving all over God's green earth to get them where they need to be.) Once they turn sixteen—forget it! The money alone for my teenager to drive will most likely result in a modification for us. I just can't afford it with the money my ex is paying me. It's been ten years!

—Carrie

By the time we got to mediation and settlement options my bank account was empty. I honestly didn't have any more money to pay my attorney, and I was ready to be done with the divorce and move on. I gave in to the initial custody and child support proposal, not really prepared for what was to come. A year later I was calling family members and asking for financial help while my husband was putting the finishing touches on the "man cave" in his basement, complete with flat screen TVs, a wet bar, and leather movie theater seating. Must be nice, I thought. The trouble was, he was paying me exactly what he was supposed to pay me.

I hadn't calculated properly that my lifestyle as a single mom with three kids would cost more than my child support and income from my part-time job could or would provide. Working a full-time job would have been impossible, especially with three kids under the age of ten at home. The cost of childcare alone would have been more than my salary, so I didn't know what to do. Since I hadn't calculated our living expenses correctly, and couldn't afford to hire an attorney, I had to go through the child support office to request a modification. (Talk about a pain in the ass!)

Eventually we were able to reach an agreement with modifications to better support my children and me, but it took a large amount of time, energy, and effort on my part. If I could give anyone advice, it would be to get it right the first time. Yes, you might be broke right now and not able to pay your attorney for more time to fight for reasonable child support, but it's smarter to pay him/her now than have to revisit an attorney a year from now (and attempt to survive with children on a budget you can't realistically live on).

—Michelle

Reading Carrie's story, you can understand her frustration and challenges with growing kids and changing budgets. You can't control the future, but you can control the present. We can't emphasize this enough: don't get screwed by settling quickly and agreeing to custody and child support that will not sufficiently take care of you or your children!

Yes, it is your attorney's job to watch closely and advise to the best of their ability what your future should look like, but ultimately it's your butt on the line. If you haven't adequately mapped out your budget the time is now! (Actually, it's past due, but we're being nice because you're our girlfriend.)

Let's say you "goofed" the first time around and you want to request a modification in child support. What are your next steps?

Every state is different when it comes to divorce and child support laws, but the basic outline usually stays the same:

- You will need to provide grounds for the modification request—documenting a significant change in circumstances (loss of job, change in income, change in cost of living, change in custody, etc.).

- Some states require a certain amount of time to pass before requesting modification (i.e., a request for review can only be made every two years after the last request or proceeding went through the courts).
- Modifications will process through your state's official child support division.

To check the laws where you live, google "child support modification," then add your state.

Top Five Things to Remember About Child Support

1. Unless it's on paper and legally documented, it doesn't count.
2. Don't rely on his promises to "trust" that he will pay you.
3. Make sure your expenses are accurate and you've accounted for the growing changes of your family over time.
4. If he doesn't pay you, run, skip, jump, hop as fast as you can to the nearest child support services office.
5. If your child support reward is not enough to truly support your children, take the steps necessary to make modifications as quickly as possible.

Will He Have to Pay Me Alimony? If so, How Much and for How Long?

Not every divorce results in alimony being paid. It usually depends on which state you reside in, how long you were married, and what your respective incomes are. If you've been married a short period of time and/or earn similar incomes, you may not be rewarded with alimony. However, if you've dedicated a significant number of years to your marriage (usually ten or more), or put your career on hold to be a homemaker/wife to raise your children and/or to be a wife, and/or do not make enough money to support yourself without additional financial resources, then you will most likely receive some sort of alimony.

Each state has its own requirements, but, if allowed, alimony (or spousal support) usually comes into play when one spouse is truly unable to support themselves without financial assistance from the other spouse. Additionally, alimony typically is awarded for a specific number of years.

If you don't have children and earn comparable salaries, you can most likely expect a 50/50 division of assets with little or no spousal support to be required.

If you've been married for twenty years, haven't had a job in fifteen, and have four kids running around the house, chances are your alimony will provide for your lack of income (the chances of you being able to get a job to fully support yourself and four children are slim) and the expenses required to maintain a decent lifestyle for you and your children.

Alimony cases are decided on by a judge. Just as each divorce and situation is different, so is each judge, as Captain Carol pointed out. Your attorney should be able to give you a snapshot of what you can (or shouldn't) expect from alimony.

It's also important to understand that alimony is received under the conditions that you are unable to live without the financial support of your ex-spouse. Just like child support, if your circumstances change, your alimony is subject to modification and/or termination. When it comes to termination, alimony usually stops after a designated amount of time (say three to seven years) and is normally effectuated on a sliding scale down. Another factor to consider is, oftentimes when the person receiving support remarries or enters a domestic partnership, (a live-in boyfriend could also provide grounds for termination—just one of many reasons to stay single for a while!) verbiage is normally included in your settlement agreement that will make this grounds for immediate termination of any and all alimony payments.

One other suggestion for alimony is the lump-sum payment. This is an especially enticing option if you know there are savings, retirement, and accounts that qualify to be withdrawn against or set up funds within to provide for spousal maintenance when your ex may not actually have the month-to-month income to help you right now, despite your need. Valerie took this option in a QDRO after realizing the money just wasn't there monthly; however, there were funds she was entitled to that she would be able to tap into as a form of lump-sum alimony. Added bonus: every month her ex didn't have to write a check and cringe. It was set up once, the funds were transferred, and he never had to hear about it again.

In a Nutshell

While a quick and seamless divorce settlement seems like the easiest option, we can't emphasize this enough: do not settle for anything less than you deserve.

There are so many details to be aware of, especially when there are minor children, property, and significant income and expenses to explore. The details of each category are so important, so take your time, do your homework, ask as many questions as you can, and consult with your attorney on things you don't understand.

One small oversight or mistake on your part could end up costing you thousands and thousands of dollars (not to mention years of struggle).

Don't sign on that dotted line until you feel 100 percent confident in your settlement agreement, especially if you are going through court-ordered or independent mediation. Truly think about the terms you are agreeing to; there are no take-backs once both parties have signed. Trust us, although mediation may feel informal, it is anything but. Once you have a signed agreement, whether agreed upon and signed in or outside of mediation, you better be okay with what it looks like for a minimum of two to three years.

Your well-being and the well-being of your children are at stake. Remember, your attorney's job is to get you the best settlement possible, but at the end of the day you're the one who will have to live with it.

Which leads us to our final discussion . . .

Negotiation

"Don't bargain yourself down before you get to the table."

—Carol Frohlinger

When we say "don't settle," we don't mean "don't settle ever or on anything." We just mean don't settle for less than your trusted intuition is telling you to! As ex-wives we have been through it, seen it, and survived it. You will, too.

But just like anything else in this world, you must be open to some sort of negotiation. If you're entering this divorce with a mindset of "I'm gonna kill him in court," you might (okay, definitely) need to take a breather. And we say that in the most loving and supportive kind of way, of course. ☺

Negotiations are an important and essential part of coming to a settlement agreement, because, ultimately, your goal is to reach an agreement that BOTH of you can (gasp) agree on.

Unless, of course, your soon-to-be ex is a saint from heaven and will happily agree to whatever you want. (In that case, can you send us his contact info?)

> *My counselor once said something very wise to me about why spouses hate negotiating. She said the problem was nobody liked half a pie when they were used to having the whole pie. And she was right. Every time I went grocery shopping at Publix I would just stare at the sad little half pies in the grocery store that only women with twenty cats bought on a Friday night at 9:59 p.m., a minute before the store closed so nobody would see them. A half pie sucks. Its edges are rough and something is just missing. Especially when you can see how beautiful the whole pie looks.*
>
> —Valerie

On a serious note . . . while you may be feeling attacked, vulnerable, angry, guilty, or anxious, you must check your emotions at the door. Lean in, channel your inner Sheryl Sandberg, and think of your divorce as a business transaction. Negotiations happen in almost everything when there's an exchange of something valuable (although that isn't to say we don't negotiate daily popsicles for clean bedrooms). Right now you have the ball, so don't give it up without a fight.

There's also an important lesson to be learned here. If you are unreasonable, and appear to be impossible for negotiating, the process will get ugly. And then uglier. There comes a point in time where you have to put the weapons down and agree to disagree.

Mediation

Divorce is the dissolution of a marital agreement. You may or may not want a divorce, but when you've found yourself at the mediation table with your attorney, their attorney, and Satan himself, the divorce is happening, whether you like it or not.

Now is not the time to cry or have a meltdown. (That's what your friends are for, and we are here for you, too!) Put your big girl panties on and get down to business.

Mediation (court-appointed or independent) should be described as the place where the negotiations will start, unless your attorneys can reach an agreement outside of court. In our experience, mediation just downright stinks. It is where the gloves first come off, and you're blindsided by the unexpected left and right hooks that are flying all over the ring.

In order to prepare yourself, have a list of your "nonnegotiables." And no, your list can't include everything, as we stated in previous chapters. Sorry, girlfriend, we know. Your nonnegotiable list should be three to five items you absolutely will not budge on.

Good examples of a nonnegotiable list would be:

- you keep the house
- the kids remain in the private school they have been attending
- your ex pays for all incurred attorney fees
- you are entitled to half of all marital 401(k) retirement account assets
- your ex takes on all joint credit card debt as his obligation

Regardless of what terms you deem nonnegotiable, have them listed on paper and share these wishes with your attorney well in advance of mediation. Your attorney needs to be prepared on what he/she really needs to go to bat on for you.

Your attorney will also advise you on what they think is reasonable during mediations. (But don't have long-winded discussions with them about this because it will cost you a bloody fortune. You are paying by the hour here for your attorney as well as the mediator.)

Valerie and her high-priced lawyer just sat there in the cramped, court-appointed room with all parties present staring at the desk while her ex and his attorney forked over collated, stapled, and printed handouts. Talk about a big old WTF moment. There it was, their well-thought-out snapshot of the current financial situation as well as an Excel spreadsheet of the points of contention they (Valerie's ex and his attorney) wanted to discuss. They were prepared to dig in and address the issues he wanted addressed and steer the negotiations toward the figures he wanted to draw attention to. She and her attorney were not.

Rather than a balanced, joint mediation, they spent eight hours following his agenda, leaving her shocked, unprepared, and somewhat screwed.

Although her attorney kept saying things like, "If you go before a court they are most likely going to rule this way anyway," and "You don't really have the money to go to court so just do what you have to do," Valerie knew what was going on didn't feel right. She was also told horror stories of so-called recent cases, which she knew were meant to scare her into submission so all parties could tick off boxes and move forward.

The funny part is Valerie did agree to things that she swore to herself and her attorney were her deal breakers. Not because she wanted to, but because she just wanted the whole thing to be over: the divorce, the harassment, the expenses, and the f'ing nightmare of a mediation.

At one point the mediator told her, "You know what, you've agreed to a lot. They need to start agreeing to some things. Let me go in and talk with them again and I'll be right back." How do you respond to that besides drop your mouth open and wish there was a bottle of tequila in front of you?

Ex-Wives' Tip:

Have a short and concise list handy and prepared. List all of the premarital assets as well as the marital assets. Make sure to list all the current debts and financial obligations. You should have a firm income number to share at this time. Put all of this on a reference sheet or Excel spreadsheet clearly coding what the "snapshot" scenario is for the mediator. This will be invaluable.

Because Valerie felt utterly unprepared emotionally, as well as in the business sense, for what was unfolding right in front of her, she acted in rash ways, dropping her boundaries left and right, which ultimately had harsh consequences. She knew in her gut most of what she agreed to just felt wrong. The mediator kept telling her, "Whenever you compromise it's not going to feel fully right; that goes against human nature."

Most importantly, once that mediator signs what you will ultimately agree on with your ex, consider it written in stone, and at least for a while on things like custody and support. During mediation you don't have to agree on everything, however, the goal is to agree on as many things as possible to keep you from having to go to court and prolonging your divorce case.

Mediation is a safeguard of sorts so that one spouse can't continue to drag out the inevitable. We get that, but it shouldn't cause you to make emotional decisions that are not in your best interest.

Mediation will form the fibers of the fabric of your settlement agreement, so make sure it is tightly knit, but not so tight that it chokes you.

Signed, Stamped, Delivered

Everything in life is negotiable, divorce settlements included. Your attorney's job is to negotiate on your behalf to get you the best settlement possible. Be reasonable. Keep your cool. You will not get everything you want. That's just not reality.

Don't let your emotions get the best of you. Be a duck if you have to at that mediation table (appear cool on the surface and kick your legs all you want under that table). Waddle away for a minute or two to really digest what you both would be legally agreeing to.

When you take the emotions out of your divorce, chances are you and your attorney will be able to find a middle ground to agree on with the opposing side. Whether they're sitting across the table from you two feet away or are in separate offices miles away, a middle ground can be found.

We know all of this is somewhat scary and overwhelming. We know you're probably reading this and thinking, *Oh. My. God. This is really happening.* Yes, it is. But the good news is this won't kill you. You will survive this just like you survived the seventh grade and all of its awfulness. And this time with better skin.

Just be prepared, stay firm on the nonnegotiables, and be rational about everything else. If you do this, your final settlement agreement will reflect something that you both can live with.

We are in no way implying that you will be jumping around asking strangers to give you a high five (okay, maybe you will on signing day). However, you no longer have to be concerned with what might be; you can now fully accept what is. Despite what you may feel today, we promise you, you will be relieved once it is over and official so you can move forward with your new life as a single woman again.

Shine On!

{how to get your groove back}

"If you're brave enough to say goodbye,
life will reward you with a new hello."

—Paulo Coelho

Congratulations! You've made it to the final chapter of our book. Let's celebrate with new beginnings, shall we?

Our goal in writing *The Ex-Wives' Guide to Divorce* was to prepare women with the knowledge and tools they need to survive divorce. But, ultimately, we also wanted to be a glimmer of hope, a little dose of happy, and a ray of sunshine through the darkness of the process.

We have armed you with the information you need to prepare and protect yourself. Now it's time for us to remind you how to love yourself.

We've heard it a million times . . . if you don't love yourself, then how can you expect someone else to love you? Well, if you don't know how to love yourself, it makes for a tricky situation.

Loving yourself isn't easy. As women, we tend to focus on our flaws, flood our brain with negative self-talk ("I am so fat!"), and shy away from compliments. What's the deal with our lack of self-confidence? Chances are, if there were a magic self-confidence pill to solve the problem it would be on the market by now (and we would have already purchased it).

If you're one of those women who has total inner peace about your life, your body, your being as a whole, then all we can say is: You go, girl! For the rest of us, there's some work to be done.

Divorce can take a serious toll on your self-confidence, but only if you allow it to. We are living proof that there IS a light at the end of the tunnel. You can, and you will, find happiness in your life again. And you may even fall in love again (hopefully with yourself first, though). While there isn't exactly a road map for getting your groove back, we certainly have some tips for you.

The Ex-Wives' Top Ten Tips for Getting Your Groove Back:

1. Take care of yourself first

Sleep. Exercise. Eat well. Limit your alcohol intake (a margarita at happy hour can be a groove-booster, but numbing yourself with a bottle of wine every night is a serious problem). It's time to take care of you. Stop worrying about everyone else. Obviously, this doesn't imply you should neglect your children, your family, or the pet goldfish. After all, it's much easier to take care of someone else than to face the reality of our own problems. Put that thong back on and step in front of the mirror to strut your stuff. You wore your big girl panties well. We are officially giving you permission to now be selfish. Consider this time in your life as a special gift to your future self.

2. Do things that make you happy

Far too often we lose ourselves in our marriage. Whether it's a hobby, a sport, playing Bunco, or taking long bubble baths . . . get back on the wagon! Dust off your tennis racquet, break out the yarn and knit a blanket, do whatever it is that makes you smile. It's your turn now.

3. Get inspired

Make a collage. All you need is a glue stick, scissors, poster board, and a stack of magazines. Cut out pictures, quotes, anything that inspires you. You may even get crafty and make a board for different categories. This exercise is fun to do with a group of girlfriends; trust us, we've done this together on several occasions!

4. Buy new bedding

This is an absolute must. While we are firm believers in responsible budget management, we also believe you should include this expense in your divorce budget. New sheets equals new woman in bed. Need we say more?

5. Update your playlists

Ditch the sappy love songs and channel your inner Beyoncé. Check out The Ex-Wives' Playlist at the end of this chapter (iTunes will be your new best friend for a while).

6. Give yourself a makeover

If you've got the money in your budget, hire someone to help. Don't freak out or roll your eyes, this is not Teen Vogue advice. This is tried and true advice, and will continue to be for many years to come. Whether it's a chic new haircut, a new pair of jeans that lift and tuck, or an updated lipstick color, even the smallest change can make a world of difference in your confidence. When you look good, you feel good. Investing in your appearance is an investment in your self-confidence, and that is the end goal, right?

7. Break up with negative people

You become like the five people you spend the most time with. Choose carefully. Who are you personally spending time with? Ever heard the phrase "misery loves company?" It's true. In order to get your groove back, you must surround yourself with people who've got the groove! If your friends are consistently Debbie Downers, then it's time for new friends. We're hoping you already did this at some point during your divorce, but if you didn't, we're giving you permission to get out there and find some shiny, happy new people to match your shiny, happy new life.

8. Unplug

Ten years ago our lives were not interrupted by text messages, Facebook alerts, emails, or the desire to snap (and post) pictures twenty-four seven on Instagram. Nowadays we're expected to respond immediately to these alerts, beeps, vibrations, etc., from our phones and electronic devices. We "multitask" (a.k.a. text, check Facebook, take iPhone pics) while grocery shopping, having lunch with friends, and so on (but never driving because we are smart girls). The sad truth is this: we're doing so many things at the same time that we aren't living in the moment. When was the last time you just left your phone at home or kept it in your car during lunch with a friend? While it might not be possible to "disconnect" all day (wouldn't that be nice?), there's significant value in unplugging, especially while spending time with your kids or right before bedtime. By removing the distraction of our so-called "smart" devices and unplugging from the outside world, you allow yourself time to connect within. And this, girlfriend, is essential to getting your groove back, not to mention really, really smart.

9. Set goals

Even the smallest of victories can be an instant pick-me-up. When it comes to post-divorce goals, you must set yourself up for success rather than failure. Maybe you've dreamed about a two-month adventure to Australia using your budgeted savings from last year. It's a great goal, but this probably isn't the best time for you to run off to Australia (just a hunch). Instead of aiming for world peace, or an entire financial makeover, let's start small. Here are some daily goals that are easily attainable with some commitment from you:

Daily *Goals*:

- Get dressed. This includes shoes, hair, and makeup.
- Make your bed—this will make you especially happy after you've purchased new bedding and fancy pillows!
- Write in a gratitude journal. This can be a simple notebook with a list of things you're thankful for each day. Simple gratitude can go a long way.
- Every night, write a list of the six most important things you need to do the next day. Do the hardest thing first.

10. Have faith

"Accept what is, let go of what was, and have faith in what will be."

—Sonia Ricotti

Regardless of your religious background or beliefs, faith is what will carry you through the trenches, the valleys, and the disappointments that seem to be inevitable during divorce. Whether it's through prayer, meditation, yoga, underwater basket weaving, whatever, this is a critical time for re-centering your energy. We challenge you to retrain your brain by bombarding it with positive affirmations. Feelings of self-worth will come along during this process, but the main goal is and should ideally be to start seeing the positive side in each circumstance. On average, it takes about sixty days to form a habit. Commit to daily positive affirmations (for example, I fill this day with hope, and I face it with joy) and you'll be amazed at the change that will come.

The Ex-Wives' Playlist

(Because, after all, divorce is the ultimate breakup)

- "Roar," Katy Perry
- "Survivor," Destiny's Child
- "We Are Never Ever Getting Back Together," Taylor Swift
- "Fighter," Christina Aguilera
- "Stronger," Britney Spears (Sorry, Holiday just can't have an awesome playlist without some Brit Brit on there!)
- "Stronger," Kelly Clarkson
- "You Oughta Know," Alanis Morissette
- "Wide Awake," Katy Perry
- "Payphone," Maroon 5
- "Irreplaceable," Beyoncé
- "Single Ladies," Beyoncé (Sorry, Valerie just can't have an awesome playlist without Queen Bey represented twice!)
- "King of Anything," Sara Bareilles
- "Wings," Little Mix
- "Respect," Aretha Franklin
- "Respect Yourself," Madonna (See the pattern here about respect?!)
- "Unwritten," Natasha Bedingfield

- "Soak Up the Sun," Sheryl Crow
- "Someone Like You," Adele (just go ahead, cry it out)

Be Selfish. It's Your Turn.

It's pretty easy to lose sight of yourself during a divorce. In fact, sometimes it's almost easier to take the focus off yourself and put it on others. This eliminates the need to face your reality. Once you've moved through the stages of grief and have arrived at the place of acceptance, we greatly encourage you to find solace in caring for yourself.

For far too long you've focused on taking care of others, whether it's your spouse, your children, your friends, etc. Make a vow here and now to yourself to be selfish.

Focus on you, what makes you happy, what brings you joy, and the vision you have for your life.

Only then will you have the clarity and peace you need as you move forward with the next chapter of your life.

Everything will be okay, and this too shall pass. Repeat it again. Everything will be okay, and this too shall pass.

Program it in your phone, plaster it on the fridge, write a Post-it to stick smack-dab in the middle of your bathroom mirror. Do whatever you have to do to remind yourself that you and millions of other women are going through, or have gone through, the same thing. Everything. Will. Be. Okay.

This is not the end of your life, but rather the beginning of the life you never thought you would live—gratefully accept the challenge and honor.

Just because our stories sometimes start without us, doesn't mean they need to end without us stealing the pen back.

Although you are no longer wearing a rock doesn't mean you don't rock, and just because your relationship failed, that does not mean you have failed as a human being. Remember these two things and repeat them daily. They will remind you of what a uniquely wonderful person you are and to be kind to yourself. Because, girlfriend, if there's one thing we do know, it's that you shine brighter than any diamond you could ever wear on your finger.

Acknowledgments

First and foremost, we would both like to thank the many incredible women who helped contribute to the content and success of this book. Your stories and encouragement not only helped to shape our book, but also our lives. We would wholeheartedly like to thank Attorney Carol Baskin and Dr. Sheri Siegel for sharing their many years of expertise as well as insight to help provide invaluable advice to our readers. We are very grateful for your contributions. A tremendous thank-you goes to our agent, Roger Williams, who believed in the two tall blonde ex-wives that shared an ex-husband, liked to talk, laughed often, and had a vision that you helped bring to life. We will be forever in your debt. To our editor, Brooke Rockwell, and the Skyhorse team, thank you for taking a chance on our project from the heart. And lastly, we would like to thank our ex-husband(s), because without you, this book would not exist.

Valerie would like to personally thank:

My mother, who showed me that even when life knocks you on your butt, the only choice you have is to jump right back up and give it all you've got. I owe my resiliency and gratitude to you.

My sweet and empathetic little boy Honey Bee, who is by far the best souvenir from the worst trip of my life. I owe you more than you will ever know for being the reason I wear a smile each and every single day of my life.

My forever friends: AE, KOH, BT, CC, GB, SB, JC, HH, MH, HM, and KA. You're all, simply put, the best. We'll always be friends because you know too much.

My co-author, for teaching me to appreciate hot pink, snow days, and that friendships sometimes come to us in the most unexpected ways. Holiday, the world is a better place with you in it.

God and the Universe, for always showing me the signs (even though I don't always pay attention) and for giving me a second chance in life. I promise I won't waste it.

Holiday would like to personally thank:

Elizabeth and Kennedy, my reasons for never giving up.

My parents, for their example of strength, dignity, and grace, even through divorce.

My husband, Clay, for loving me unconditionally, embracing and supporting me during this project, and most of all for showing me there can be a light (and even rainbows) at the end of a very dark tunnel.

My sister, Meredith, and my amazing girlfriends . . . for listening, laughing, and crying with me through it all . . . you know who you are :)

Valerie, the greatest ex-wife a woman could ever know. I could not have survived my divorce without you. Thank you for taking me under your wing and showing me the way . . . I love you!

And to God, for the divine opportunity to share my testimony with the world.

Resources

We've gathered all the handy-dandy forms, worksheets, and checklists and put them on the following pages as well as on *The Ex-Wives' Guide to Divorce* website: www.exwivesguide.com. Now everything you need to **get organized** and help prepare you for the next chapter in your life is right at your fingertips.

- Accounts Record
- Budget Worksheet
- Child Expenses Worksheet
- Child Support Payment Log
- Communication Log
- Documents Checklist
- Extracurricular Expenses Worksheet
- Personal Expenses Worksheet
- Personal Income Worksheet
- Questions for the Attorney
- To-Do List

Documents Checklist

To ensure you have copies of all your documents as you **Get Organized**, use this handy checklist.

Utilities

- ☐ Gas/oil bills
- ☐ Electric bills
- ☐ Water bills
- ☐ Cable bills
- ☐ Internet bills
- ☐ Landline and wireless phone bills

Revolving and Installment

- ☐ Credit cards (joint, personal, and business if applicable)
- ☐ Mortgage statements
- ☐ Home equity line of credit statements
- ☐ Lease (if you are renting)
- ☐ Last two years of property and vehicle tax bills
- ☐ Secured loans
- ☐ Unsecured loans
- ☐ Family loans
- ☐ Automobile loans
- ☐ Medical bills
- ☐ Other fixed payments

Financial

- ☐ Checking account statements
- ☐ Savings account statements
- ☐ Investment account statements
- ☐ Retirement account statements (401(k), IRA, etc.)
- ☐ Stocks and bonds
- ☐ Annuities
- ☐ Mutual funds statements
- ☐ 529 college savings plan statements
- ☐ Medical savings account statements
- ☐ Children's savings account statements

- ☐ Copy of any trusts
- ☐ Amount of cash on hand

Employment/Income/Self-Employed Business

- ☐ Pay stubs for the past sixty days
- ☐ The past two to five years of filed tax returns (personal, joint, business)
- ☐ Past two years; bonus or commission statements
- ☐ Additional perks/benefits (car allowance, etc.)
- ☐ Business expenses (reimbursed and non-reimbursed)
- ☐ Accounts receivable
- ☐ Accounts payable
- ☐ Profit and loss statement for the past six months
- ☐ Twelve months of business bank statements (more if deemed necessary)
- ☐ Existing contracts
- ☐ Stock options

Personal

- ☐ Birth certificates
- ☐ Social security cards for every family member
- ☐ Passports for every family member
- ☐ Driver's licenses for every family member
- ☐ Marriage license (we're hoping you haven't burned it quite yet)
- ☐ Life insurance policies
- ☐ Will
- ☐ Health, dental, and vision insurance cards

Deeds/Titles

- ☐ Car titles
- ☐ Boat, RV, etc. titles
- ☐ Deed to home
- ☐ Deed to other properties or land owned

Appraised Assets

- ☐ Jewelry appraisals
- ☐ Artwork appraisals
- ☐ Collection appraisals
- ☐ Appraisals of other high-value items

Miscellaneous

- ☐ Gym memberships
- ☐ Club memberships (country club, Costco, Bon Jovi fan club)
- ☐ Season tickets
- ☐ Organization memberships (museums, zoo, etc.)
- ☐ Frequent flyer miles
- ☐ Gift certificates
- ☐ Loyalty memberships (hotels, rental cars, DSW shoes, etc.)

To Do List

Month: ______________ **Year:** ______________

TODAY'S DATE	DUE DATE	ITEM	NOTES	FOLLOW UP NEEDED?
				☐ YES: ______ ☐ NO
				☐ YES: ______ ☐ NO
				☐ YES: ______ ☐ NO
				☐ YES: ______ ☐ NO
				☐ YES: ______ ☐ NO
				☐ YES: ______ ☐ NO
				☐ YES: ______ ☐ NO
				☐ YES: ______ ☐ NO
				☐ YES: ______ ☐ NO
				☐ YES: ______ ☐ NO
				☐ YES: ______ ☐ NO

TODAY'S DATE	DUE DATE	ITEM	NOTES	FOLLOW UP NEEDED?
				☐ YES: ______ ☐ NO
				☐ YES: ______ ☐ NO
				☐ YES: ______ ☐ NO
				☐ YES: ______ ☐ NO
				☐ YES: ______ ☐ NO
				☐ YES: ______ ☐ NO
				☐ YES: ______ ☐ NO
				☐ YES: ______ ☐ NO
				☐ YES: ______ ☐ NO
				☐ YES: ______ ☐ NO
				☐ YES: ______ ☐ NO

Questions for Attorney

CONCERN/ISSUE	QUESTION	ANSWER	ACTIONS NEEDED FOR SOLUTION
Child Support	*Can I have child support deducted from his paycheck so I don't have to chase him down every week? If so, what do I need to do to start the process?*	*YES*	**I NEED TO:** document late payments **ATTORNEY WILL:** contact child support collection agency/office and provide supporting documents to initiate paycheck deduction.

CONCERN/ISSUE	QUESTION	ANSWER	ACTIONS NEEDED FOR SOLUTION

Child Support Payment Log

Month: ____________ **Year:** ____________

DATE DUE	DATE RECEIVED	CHECK NUMBER	SUPPORT OWED	SUPPORT PAID	PAYMENT PERIOD	BALANCE	NOTES

DATE DUE	DATE RECEIVED	CHECK NUMBER	SUPPORT OWED	SUPPORT PAID	PAYMENT PERIOD	BALANCE	NOTES

Communication Log

Records of communication with:

- ☐ Spouse/Ex
- ☐ Attorney
- ☐ School/Teacher/Childcare
- ☐ Other: ______________________

DATE	TYPE OF COMMUNICATION (phone, text, email, letter, in-person conversation)	REASON FOR COMMUNICATION	NOTES/DETAILS
2/14/13	Email- received	Last minute change in schedule	Received email at 3pm "cancelling" plan to have child for evening. His scheduled pick up time was 5pm. Had to leave work early to pick up child from daycare.

DATE	TYPE OF COMMUNICATION (phone, text, email, letter, in-person conversation)	REASON FOR COMMUNICATION	NOTES/DETAILS

Personal Income

Month: ________________ **Year:** ________

DATE	AMOUNT PAID	PAYMENT METHOD (cash, check, direct deposit, other)	DEPOSIT DATE	DESCRIPTION/NOTES/DETAILS
4/1/13	$1,067.25	Direct deposit	3/30/13	Bi-monthly paycheck

DATE	AMOUNT PAID	PAYMENT METHOD (*cash, check, direct deposit, other*)	DEPOSIT DATE	DESCRIPTION/NOTES/DETAILS

Personal Expenses

Month: ______________ **Year:** ________

DATE	AMOUNT	PAYMENT METHOD	DESCRIPTION/DETAILS	POSSIBLE REIMBURSEMENT?	NOTES
4/1/13	$300.00	☐ Cash ☐ Check #: ☐ C.C. Acct #: ☒ Auto Pay Bank Acct #: ends in 6789	Car payment	☒ NO ☐ PARTIALLY ☐ ENTIRELY	Recurring bill on 1st of month from checking account
		☐ Cash ☐ Check #: ☐ C.C. Acct #: ☐ Auto Pay Bank Acct #:		☐ NO ☐ PARTIALLY ☐ ENTIRELY	
		☐ Cash ☐ Check #: ☐ C.C. Acct #: ☐ Auto Pay Bank Acct #:		☐ NO ☐ PARTIALLY ☐ ENTIRELY	
		☐ Cash ☐ Check #: ☐ C.C. Acct #: ☐ Auto Pay Bank Acct #:		☐ NO ☐ PARTIALLY ☐ ENTIRELY	
		☐ Cash ☐ Check #: ☐ C.C. Acct #: ☐ Auto Pay Bank Acct #:		☐ NO ☐ PARTIALLY ☐ ENTIRELY	
		☐ Cash ☐ Check #: ☐ C.C. Acct #: ☐ Auto Pay Bank Acct #:		☐ NO ☐ PARTIALLY ☐ ENTIRELY	
		☐ Cash ☐ Check #: ☐ C.C. Acct #: ☐ Auto Pay Bank Acct #:		☐ NO ☐ PARTIALLY ☐ ENTIRELY	
		☐ Cash ☐ Check #: ☐ C.C. Acct #: ☐ Auto Pay Bank Acct #:		☐ NO ☐ PARTIALLY ☐ ENTIRELY	
		☐ Cash ☐ Check #: ☐ C.C. Acct #: ☐ Auto Pay Bank Acct #:		☐ NO ☐ PARTIALLY ☐ ENTIRELY	
		☐ Cash ☐ Check #: ☐ C.C. Acct #: ☐ Auto Pay Bank Acct #:		☐ NO ☐ PARTIALLY ☐ ENTIRELY	
		☐ Cash ☐ Check #: ☐ C.C. Acct #: ☐ Auto Pay Bank Acct #:		☐ NO ☐ PARTIALLY ☐ ENTIRELY	

DATE	AMOUNT	PAYMENT METHOD	DESCRIPTION/DETAILS	POSSIBLE REIMBURSEMENT?	NOTES
		☐ Cash ☐ Check #: ☐ C.C. Acct #: ☐ Auto Pay Bank Acct #:		☐ NO ☐ PARTIALLY ☐ ENTIRELY	
		☐ Cash ☐ Check #: ☐ C.C. Acct #: ☐ Auto Pay Bank Acct #:		☐ NO ☐ PARTIALLY ☐ ENTIRELY	
		☐ Cash ☐ Check #: ☐ C.C. Acct #: ☐ Auto Pay Bank Acct #:		☐ NO ☐ PARTIALLY ☐ ENTIRELY	
		☐ Cash ☐ Check #: ☐ C.C. Acct #: ☐ Auto Pay Bank Acct #:		☐ NO ☐ PARTIALLY ☐ ENTIRELY	
		☐ Cash ☐ Check #: ☐ C.C. Acct #: ☐ Auto Pay Bank Acct #:		☐ NO ☐ PARTIALLY ☐ ENTIRELY	
		☐ Cash ☐ Check #: ☐ C.C. Acct #: ☐ Auto Pay Bank Acct #:		☐ NO ☐ PARTIALLY ☐ ENTIRELY	
		☐ Cash ☐ Check #: ☐ C.C. Acct #: ☐ Auto Pay Bank Acct #:		☐ NO ☐ PARTIALLY ☐ ENTIRELY	
		☐ Cash ☐ Check #: ☐ C.C. Acct #: ☐ Auto Pay Bank Acct #:		☐ NO ☐ PARTIALLY ☐ ENTIRELY	
		☐ Cash ☐ Check #: ☐ C.C. Acct #: ☐ Auto Pay Bank Acct #:		☐ NO ☐ PARTIALLY ☐ ENTIRELY	
		☐ Cash ☐ Check #: ☐ C.C. Acct #: ☐ Auto Pay Bank Acct #:		☐ NO ☐ PARTIALLY ☐ ENTIRELY	
		☐ Cash ☐ Check #: ☐ C.C. Acct #: ☐ Auto Pay Bank Acct #:		☐ NO ☐ PARTIALLY ☐ ENTIRELY	
		☐ Cash ☐ Check #: ☐ C.C. Acct #: ☐ Auto Pay Bank Acct #:		☐ NO ☐ PARTIALLY ☐ ENTIRELY	

Child Expenses

Ratio: ______/______
e.g. 40% (you) / 60% (spouse)

Child: ______________ **Month:**______

DATE	AMOUNT DUE	AMOUNT PAID	PAYMENT METHOD	DESCRIPTION	EXPENSE BREAKDOWN (use ratio to figure breakdown of cost & what is owed to you)	NOTES
5/16/13	$250.00	$250.00	☐ Cash ☐ Check #: 1698 ☐ C.C. Acct #: ☐ Auto Pay Bank Acct #:	Daycare: week of 5/6-5/10	$150.00 (*60% of $250)	Paid balance in full to avoid late fee.
			☐ Cash ☐ Check #: ☐ C.C. Acct #: ☐ Auto Pay Bank Acct #:			
			☐ Cash ☐ Check #: ☐ C.C. Acct #: ☐ Auto Pay Bank Acct #:			
			☐ Cash ☐ Check #: ☐ C.C. Acct #: ☐ Auto Pay Bank Acct #:			
			☐ Cash ☐ Check #: ☐ C.C. Acct #: ☐ Auto Pay Bank Acct #:			
			☐ Cash ☐ Check #: ☐ C.C. Acct #: ☐ Auto Pay Bank Acct #:			
			☐ Cash ☐ Check #: ☐ C.C. Acct #: ☐ Auto Pay Bank Acct #:			
			☐ Cash ☐ Check #: ☐ C.C. Acct #: ☐ Auto Pay Bank Acct #:			
			☐ Cash ☐ Check #: ☐ C.C. Acct #: ☐ Auto Pay Bank Acct #:			
			☐ Cash ☐ Check #: ☐ C.C. Acct #: ☐ Auto Pay Bank Acct #:			
			☐ Cash ☐ Check #: ☐ C.C. Acct #: ☐ Auto Pay Bank Acct #:			

DATE	AMOUNT DUE	AMOUNT PAID	PAYMENT METHOD	DESCRIPTION	EXPENSE BREAKDOWN *(use ratio to figure breakdown of cost & what is owed to you)*	NOTES
			☐ Cash ☐ Check #: ☐ C.C. Acct #: ☐ Auto Pay Bank Acct #:			
			☐ Cash ☐ Check #: ☐ C.C. Acct #: ☐ Auto Pay Bank Acct #:			
			☐ Cash ☐ Check #: ☐ C.C. Acct #: ☐ Auto Pay Bank Acct #:			
			☐ Cash ☐ Check #: ☐ C.C. Acct #: ☐ Auto Pay Bank Acct #:			
			☐ Cash ☐ Check #: ☐ C.C. Acct #: ☐ Auto Pay Bank Acct #:			
			☐ Cash ☐ Check #: ☐ C.C. Acct #: ☐ Auto Pay Bank Acct #:			
			☐ Cash ☐ Check #: ☐ C.C. Acct #: ☐ Auto Pay Bank Acct #:			
			☐ Cash ☐ Check #: ☐ C.C. Acct #: ☐ Auto Pay Bank Acct #:			
			☐ Cash ☐ Check #: ☐ C.C. Acct #: ☐ Auto Pay Bank Acct #:			
			☐ Cash ☐ Check #: ☐ C.C. Acct #: ☐ Auto Pay Bank Acct #:			
			☐ Cash ☐ Check #: ☐ C.C. Acct #: ☐ Auto Pay Bank Acct #:			
			☐ Cash ☐ Check #: ☐ C.C. Acct #: ☐ Auto Pay Bank Acct #:			
			☐ Cash ☐ Check #: ☐ C.C. Acct #: ☐ Auto Pay Bank Acct #:			
			☐ Cash ☐ Check #: ☐ C.C. Acct #: ☐ Auto Pay Bank Acct #:			

Extracurricular Expenses

Ratio: ______/______

*e.g. 40% (you) / 60% (spouse)

Child: ______________ **Year:**______

ACTIVITY/ EXPENSE	AMOUNT DUE	DATE DUE	AMOUNT PAID	PAYMENT METHOD (cash, check, credit card, other)	BALANCE DUE	TOTAL OWED TO ME: (use ratio to figure out your breakdown of cost & what is owed to you)	NOTES
Baseball registration	$75.00	6/1/13	$75.00	Check #1678	n/a	$45 (60% of $75)	*include total in weekly email update

ACTIVITY/ EXPENSE	AMOUNT DUE	DATE DUE	AMOUNT PAID	PAYMENT METHOD *(cash, check, credit card, other)*	BALANCE DUE	TOTAL OWED TO ME: *(use ratio to figure out your breakdown of cost & what is owed to you)*	NOTES

Accounts

ACCOUNT/WEBSITE	USERNAME	PASSWORD	EMAIL USED

	SPENT	BUDGETED
FOOD		
Groceries		
Restaurants		
CLOTHING		
Adults		
Children		
Dry Cleaning/Laundry		
HOUSING		
First Mortgage/Rent		
Second Mortgage		
Repairs/Maintenance		
Association/Dues		
UTILITIES		
Electricity		
Gas		
Water		
Trash		
Phone/Mobile		
Internet		
Cable		
Other:		
Other:		
MEDICAL		
Prescriptions		
Doctor Bills		
Dentist		
Vitamins		
Other:		

MONTHLY TAKE HOME PAY: __________

	SPENT	BUDGETED
TRANSPORTATION		
Gas		
Oil Changes		
Maintenance/Repairs		
Tires		
Other		
DEBTS		
Car Payment 1		
Car Payment 2		
Credit Card:		
Credit Card:		
Credit Card:		
Credit Card:		
Credit Card:		
Student Loan:		
Student Loan:		
Loan (Other)		
Loan (Other)		
Other		
Other		
Other		
INSURANCE		
Life Insurance		
Health Insurance		
Homeowner/Renter		
Auto Insurance		
Other		

	SPENT	BUDGETED
PERSONAL		
Child Support		
Alimony		
Child Care/Babysitter		
Baby Supplies (Diapers,		
Toiletries		
Cosmetics/Skin Care		
Hair Care/Haircuts, etc.		
Nail Care/Appointments		
Education/Tuition		
Books/Supplies		
Subscriptions		
Gym Membership		
Pet Supplies/Food/Vet		
Club/Organization Dues		
Gifts- Birthdays		
Gifts- Holidays/Occasions		
Miscellaneous		
Other:		
Other:		
Other:		
RECREATION		
Entertainment/Movies, etc.		
Vacation		
SUMMER CAMPS		
Child 1		
Child 2		
Child 3		
Child 4		

	SPENT	BUDGETED
CHARITY		
Tithes		
Charity/Offerings		
SAVINGS		
Emergency Fund		
Retirement Fund		
College Fund		
OTHER		

Add up the totals from each category and subtract from your take-home pay for a complete picture of your spending. Adjust your budget accordingly.

NOTES: